How to Design, Implement, and Analyse a Survey

Anthony Arundel

Professorial Fellow, UNU-MERIT, Maastricht University, the Netherlands

T0327461

EE **Edward Elgar**
PUBLISHING

Cheltenham, UK • Northampton, MA, USA

Published by
Edward Elgar Publishing Limited
The Lypiatts
15 Lansdown Road
Cheltenham
Glos GL50 2JA
UK

Edward Elgar Publishing, Inc.
William Pratt House
9 Dewey Court
Northampton
Massachusetts 01060
USA

Paperback edition 2024

A catalogue record for this book
is available from the British Library

Library of Congress Control Number: 2023930158

This book is available electronically in the **Elgar**online
Business subject collection
http://dx.doi.org/10.4337/9781800376175

ISBN 978 1 80037 616 8 (cased)
ISBN 978 1 80037 617 5 (eBook)
ISBN 978 1 0353 4445 1 (paperback)

Printed and bound by CPI Group (UK) Ltd, Croydon, CR0 4YY

How to Design, Implement, and Analyse a Survey

Contents

Acknowledgements

I would like to thank Nordine Es-Sadki of UNU-MERIT and Alicia Mintzes, head of research of Breville Australia, for their very useful comments on the chapters in this handbook. Additional advice on specific issues was contributed by Pierre Mohnen of UNU-MERIT and Louise Earl, formerly with Statistics Canada and currently with the Institute for Science, Society and Policy at the University of Ottawa. I would also like to acknowledge the many participants of Eurostat's Community Innovation Survey Taskforce between 2004 and 2018 for many fruitful discussions on questionnaire problems and solutions in multiple European countries. Other people who have contributed to my knowledge of questionnaire design, testing and survey implementation include Adriana van Cruysen, Kieran O'Brien, formerly at the Australian Innovation Research Centre, Fred Gault, formerly at Statistics Canada, and Sue-Ellen Luke, director at the Australian Bureau of Statistics. All errors of course, are entirely my own.

1. Introduction

This handbook is about how to conduct a questionnaire survey, from the initial steps of designing a questionnaire to answer research questions, through implementation and data cleaning, to initial data analysis. The handbook is designed to be a practical guide for undergraduate and graduate students, academics, or business managers with no survey experience at all or with some survey experience, for instance with analysing survey data but not with conducting a survey, or individuals who have conducted a survey of a small number of people but would like to undertake a larger, more extensive survey. In addition, the information in this handbook on good practices for questionnaire design and survey implementation should provide academics with the knowledge to critically evaluate the quality of survey data used in research.

All surveys are sent to individuals for completion. A common type of survey only asks individuals about themselves, such as their attitudes, preferences, voting intentions, educational or other experiences, or purchasing plans. A second approach is to ask individuals to answer questions about the organizations of which they have direct experience, either because they work for the organization, or they are a student or patient at the organization. Surveys of organizations are often directed towards managers who have the power to make decisions about strategies or who have knowledge about activities that are the subject of the questionnaire. For example, a questionnaire on innovation could be sent to the person who manages research and development activities, whereas a questionnaire on human resource policies could be sent to a manager in the human resources department. The third approach combines questions on the individual with questions on the organization. An example is a survey of PhD students, which asks each student about their own activities and career aspirations, plus questions on the organizational environment of their university (Sauermann and Roach, 2013).

You, the reader, are very likely to have completed a survey targeted to individuals. You may have responded to a survey on your voting intentions, your opinions of different political parties, or you may have been asked to answer questions on your experiences with a service, such as an airplane flight or a product that you purchased. If you have completed a tax return form you have answered a type of survey of individuals, although in many countries you are expected to find the forms yourself, rather than the forms being sent to you by post or email by the tax department. Households are organizations (albeit small ones), so you have taken part in a survey of organizations if you participated in a marketing survey that asked about the spending plans of your household or the types of products that your household currently owns, or if you completed a census form that asked for information about yourself and everyone else in your household.

A moment's reflection on individual compared to organizational surveys, perhaps based on your own experience, should lead to the conclusion that organizational surveys are more complex and face different issues than surveys of individuals. Out of multiple possibilities, who should answer an organizational survey, including a household survey? One would expect, correctly, that there must be rules for who answers. How do you identify individuals to survey within large organizations and should they answer questions only for their area of expertise?

This handbook provides guidelines for questionnaire surveys of organizations, including surveys targeted to a division, department or work team within an organization and questions on the organization or the organization and the respondent. Most of the examples are drawn from surveys of businesses, governments and non-governmental organizations (NGOs). Although this handbook rarely provides examples for surveys of households or individuals, many of the guidelines will apply to them. The main methodological difference between surveys of individuals and organizations concerns the identification of the target population and individuals to be sampled.

1.1   DO YOU NEED A SURVEY?

The first question that you need to answer is: do you need to conduct a survey? The main advantage of a survey is to create new data that are not available from other sources. This is achieved through survey questions that are specifically designed to answer your research questions. In this respect, questionnaire surveys are *research driven*.

Yet, compared to other methods of obtaining data on organizations, such as using existing data or creating new data through case studies, a series of interviews, or extracting and compiling data from the internet, surveys can be expensive. Surveys are not necessarily more difficult than other methods of creating new data, but they can be more complex and therefore require disciplined attention to detail – no skipping tasks or taking short cuts, at least without careful evaluation of the implications of a short cut for response rates and data quality. Surveys also create a 'response burden' for respondents, who must expend effort and time to complete a survey questionnaire. To minimize costs to yourself and to potential respondents, a careful evaluation of other data sources should be conducted before a decision to proceed with a survey. An evaluation of other data sources can identify data that are unavailable and consequently must be obtained from a survey, and available data that could be linked to a survey, thereby reducing costs for yourself and to respondents.

Alternative data sources include 'big' data obtained from the internet, publicly available administrative data such as patent applications, and censuses and other survey data. Sometimes microdata from previous surveys of organizations or individuals are publicly available and can be exploited for new research. Examples include the Innobarometer surveys in Europe, household surveys and national censuses, for which microdata or semi-aggregated data may be available for research purposes.

The disadvantage of alternative data sources is that they can be imperfect for your research questions. This results in *data-driven* research, requiring revisions to research questions to fit the data or heroic assumptions on what was measured by the data. Patent data, for example, are frequently used to measure innovation, but patents are not the same as innovations. Many innovations are not patented and not all patents are used in an innovation. These limitations with patents and R&D expenditures as measures of innovation partly explain the effort by the OECD and many national statistical offices to measure business innovation directly through specialized innovation surveys (OECD/Eurostat, 2018). A far too common problem with data-driven research occurs when researchers are tempted to misinterpret the questions used to obtain data to make them fit the requirements of their research questions.

A second advantage of conducting a survey, in comparison to other methods of collecting new data on organizations, such as case studies, interviews or internet data, is generalizability. Surveys that are representative of a population can produce results that are generalizable to the sampled population and sometimes to similar populations that were not sampled (Gobo, 2004). A third advantage of a survey is that they can collect sufficient data to conduct statistical analyses of relationships between variables.

Nevertheless, the three advantages of a survey need to be weighed against their disadvantages in terms of the necessary funding and effort to obtain good results. Even if alternative data sources are imperfect, it may be worthwhile to accept the limitations of data-driven research and adjust your research questions to fit existing data instead of designing and implementing a new survey.

If a survey is the only way that you will be able to obtain the data you need, there are still options for reducing the cost and effort required. It may be possible to answer your research questions through a small census of all organizations with specific characteristics of interest to your research. Small censuses with fewer than 300–500 sampled individuals are considerably less expensive and require less effort than large surveys based on a probability sample.

There are two other factors that you need to consider before proceeding with a survey. First, you need to know if you have sufficient funding. This requires estimating the survey cost, particularly if you will apply for a grant to fund your survey. At UNU-MERIT in the Netherlands, we estimated the *non-personnel* costs of a combined postal–online survey at 15 Euros per returned questionnaire in 2019. This covered the cost of envelopes, paper, printing the questionnaire and postage for all individuals in the sample, including those who did not respond. Your non-personnel costs may be higher or lower, depending on your topic, location and the characteristics of your sample. Personnel costs, if separately funded, are always much higher than the non-personnel costs.

You may already have a solution that you have heard about to lower survey costs – conduct a survey online! Although considerable personnel time is still required to identify individuals to receive the questionnaire, an entirely online survey substantially reduces non-personnel and other personnel costs, but often at the expense of lower response rates. In an environment where obtaining a good response rate is difficult, you may need to pay more to get more.

Second, you need to consider time limitations, with a combined online–postal survey of approximately eight pages in length taking approximately six months. This includes a minimum of two months to design and test a questionnaire while simultaneously constructing a sample, three months when the survey is in the field and one month for post-survey activities such as data cleaning. Less time is required for shorter questionnaires, which are also less expensive per response, and for interview-based surveys conducted by telephone, which are more expensive. Another constraint is that the three months when the survey is underway ('in the field') should not overlap with major holiday periods or times when people go on vacation. In many countries in the Northern Hemisphere, the survey should not be in the field between mid-December and mid-January nor during July and August. In several countries in the Southern Hemisphere, surveys should not be conducted between early December and late January. Before late December potential respondents are likely to be enticed by a continuous flow of pre-holiday parties and from early to mid or late January by their vacations.

1.2   IDENTIFYING GOOD PRACTICES

This handbook provides guidelines for good practices for the design and implementation of a questionnaire based on the author's extensive personal experience with multiple surveys of organizations in Europe and Australia and a review of published research in this field. With rare exceptions, such as the need for testing questionnaires, this handbook does not refer to 'best practices' because they seldom exist, due to differences in context such as cultural differences across countries, constraints such as a lack of funds that limit what is possible, or a lack of good empirical evidence supporting one practice over another.

Much of the published research that is cited in this book uses high-quality experimental designs to compare different survey methods. These include techniques to encourage sampled individuals to complete and return a survey questionnaire, evaluations of the differences in the quality of data obtained through different survey methods (online, mailed, face-to-face interviews, or telephone interviews), or methods to detect poor-quality responses. The disadvantage of the published research is that a large share of these studies used surveys of the opinions and perceptions of individuals on a range of issues, such as their voting intentions or their experiences with products. Very few experimental studies focused on managers or professionals who are often the target of organizational surveys. In addition, a large share of the experimental research draws on university students or paid commercial panels in English-speaking countries, predominantly the United States, though a few studies have been conducted in countries that speak other languages (Revilla and Ochoa, 2014). Although this research provides useful pointers to good practice, the disadvantage is that young university students or the participants of paid panels are very unlikely to be representative of the managers of businesses, government agencies or NGOs.

1.3   CONCLUSIONS

To sum up, anyone thinking of conducting a survey needs to make an informed decision on whether to survey or seek other methods for acquiring data, which requires a basic understanding of what a survey requires. This is provided in Chapter 2 on survey fundamentals, which includes definitions, an overview of all necessary steps, and how to estimate a financial budget and a time budget. You may also wish to read through Chapter 3 on questionnaire design and Chapter 4 on testing your questionnaire, which is an essential requirement that cannot be skipped to save time or costs. Chapter 5 on survey implementation covers the most expensive part of the survey, which is the identification of individuals to receive your questionnaire and the delivery of the questionnaire to them. Chapter 6 covers post-survey activities to clean the data, check data quality issues and deal with non-response issues. Chapter 7 covers data analysis issues that are linked to the question design or survey method.

If you decide to conduct a survey, all chapters, including Chapter 2, are designed to provide you with sufficient knowledge to conduct a survey from translating your research questions into survey questions to data collection and analyses to prepare your data for further use. Depending on your survey design and goals, you may also want additional details on specialized topics that are not covered in this handbook. Each chapter includes references that should be of help if you want or need additional information.

A few comments on the language in this handbook are called for. Oddly, there isn't a satisfactory word to describe the individuals who are sent a survey questionnaire to complete. In this handbook I use 'sample', 'sampled individuals', 'potential respondents' and occasionally 'person', depending on the context. Finally, where possible this handbook avoids jargon, for example it refers to a 'questionnaire' instead of an 'instrument', but many concepts require technical terms. These are explained at first use and can be found in the index.

2. Survey fundamentals

2.1 INTRODUCTION

Chapter 1 may have given you the impression that designing and implementing a survey involves following a sequence of stages, such as translating your research questions into survey questions, questionnaire testing, drawing a sample, implementing the survey, post-survey data cleaning and related activities, and finally analysis. This is true, but there is another dimension that complicates the process: question design, survey implementation and data analysis are interconnected. The focal task is the design of the questionnaire, but you can't complete this task without taking into consideration the effect of other survey components, such as the survey delivery method and the statistical methods that you plan to use for data analysis. These linkages between different stages means that you can't begin the first step of translating your research questions into survey questions without knowing what else is involved at later stages. But this isn't the end of the complications that you need to consider. Two vitally important goals influence questionnaire design and implementation: the need to optimize response rates and data quality. These two goals need to be balanced with the available budget and time. Figure 2.1 provides an overview of the linkages between different survey activities and the design of the questionnaire.

Essentially, you need to read the entire handbook to design and implement a good-quality survey, but to give you a head start this chapter covers the fundamentals, the important linkages between different parts of the process, and how to estimate a budget for the costs and time required for a survey.

2.2 TYPES OF QUESTIONNAIRES AND SURVEYS

A survey can vary in size from 25 to several thousand individuals and can use open questions that ask for written or spoken responses to questions, closed questions with a limited number of fixed response options, such as 'yes' or 'no', or a combination of open and closed questions. Semi-structured questionnaires mostly contain open questions and are often implemented during a face-to-face or telephone interview, which gives the interviewer an opportunity to probe for additional information. They rarely involve more than 100

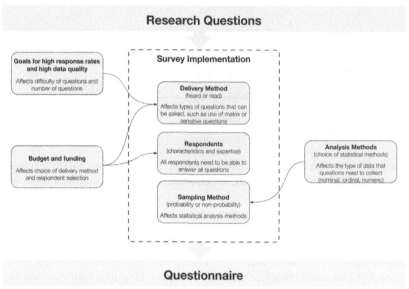

Source: Figure graphics by Alicia Mintzes.

Figure 2.1   *Factors to consider when translating research questions into*
                  a survey questionnaire

respondents because of high interview costs. Structured questionnaires mostly contain closed questions with a few open questions that ask for very brief responses of several sentences and can be sent to tens or thousands of people. Table 2.1 provides an example of two structured and one semi-structured question.

All survey types, cross-sectional, panel, semi-structured and structured, can be nested or part of a linked survey. A nested survey covers multiple individuals within each of several organizations of the same type. An example is a survey of all faculty deans in all universities in a country, where sampled individuals are nested within the larger organization of a university. A variant of the nested survey is the linked survey, where questionnaire results from individual respondents such as employees or middle managers are linked to responses from other individuals, such as the manager for each employee or senior managers. A linked survey often uses different questions for the two types of respondents. A second type of linked survey combines survey results to data from non-survey sources, either for specific respondents or for groups of respondents that share similar characteristics, for example location in the same region or part of the same industry. For instance, patent data or administrative

Table 2.1   *Examples of structured (closed) and semi-structured (open)*
                         questions

Structured		
Did your university apply for one or more patents in the last year?	Yes	☐
	No	☐
What was the total amount of patent licence income earned by your university in the last year?		_____,000 €
Semi-structured		
In your experience, what were the most important factors that influence the amount of patent licence income earned by your university?		

data on employment or sales can be linked to a survey. Data linkage from different time periods can also create a time lag with the survey variables.

Questionnaire development, implementation and post-survey data activities are similar for all types of surveys. Conversely, the statistical analysis can differ by the type of survey, with semi-structured questionnaires, panel, nested and linked surveys using different statistical methods than structured questionnaire surveys (section 7.3).

2.2.1   Causality

Both semi-structured and structured questionnaires can be part of a cross-sectional survey design or part of a panel design. A cross-sectional survey asks about events that occurred over a specified time period. This 'reference' period is usually before the date when the survey is implemented, but some questions can refer to future expectations. A panel (or longitudinal) survey collects data from the same respondents at two or more points in time.

Cross-sectional surveys are poor at establishing causality because data on both outcomes and the factors that are expected to influence outcomes are measured at the same time and often refer to the same time period. Establishing causality requires a time gap between the measurement of an event and an outcome, a correlation between causal factors and the outcome, and a plausible explanation for a causal relationship.

Nevertheless, cross-sectional data is often used to look for plausible causal relationships between variables. For instance, a plausible hypothesis is that involving citizens in the design of a new public service will improve user satisfaction with the service. However, regression analysis using cross-sectional data that confirms this hypothesis will not establish causality because user satisfaction could have impelled the designers of the service to seek user involvement – i.e. the causality could run in the opposite direction, although this is a less plausible hypothesis.

A time gap can be created artificially in a cross-sectional survey by using different reference periods within the same questionnaire. For instance, a question on inputs to innovation could cover the previous three years, while a question on sales or profits from innovation can refer to the most recent year only. Even without specified time periods, questions on inputs to an activity are likely to have occurred before the organization assessed any outcomes from the activity. Yet this solution is not perfect because respondent memory is commonly affected by telescoping and other effects that distort respondent recall of events that happened in the past (Converse and Presser, 1986; Müggenburg, 2021). Except for memorable events, respondents often remember activities as occurring closer to the present than when they happened. For example, a respondent could remember an event that occurred three years ago as occurring two years ago (Sudman and Bradburn, 1973). Perceptions of the timing of past events are also influenced by more recent experiences or respondents' emotional state at the time of replying to the survey (Müggenburg, 2021).

A panel survey overcomes memory issues by collecting data from the same respondents at two or more time periods separated by a sufficient length of time for a set of factors to influence one or more outcomes of interest. For example, a survey on employee motivation could collect data from two surveys spaced two years apart. The first could collect data on baseline measures of employee motivation and human resource strategies across organizations while the second could measure the effect of different strategies on changes in employee motivation.

2.3   RESEARCH QUESTIONS

Research questions can be addressed using a questionnaire survey alone, or a combination of a questionnaire survey and other data sources, such as linking other sources of data on business investments and income to a survey on business strategies. Structured surveys can also be part of a mixed methods study design that includes case studies or a series of semi-structured interviews. A case study can be based on desk research supplemented with multiple semi-structured interviews, but all interviews are usually focused on a similar set of activities or event within one or a few organizations, such as a study of the challenges faced by three automobile manufacturers to develop zero carbon emission cars (Pinkse et al., 2014). A series of semi-structured interviews differ from case studies by covering a larger number of organizations, for instance interviews with managers at 50 vehicle manufacturing companies.

When there is little existing evidence for research questions, case studies can be used before a survey to identify topics to cover in a questionnaire survey. Alternatively, semi-structured interviews can be implemented after analysing a survey to provide in-depth examples of issues identified in the

Table 2.2   Advantages and disadvantages of data collection methods

	Advantages	Disadvantages
Structured questionnaire survey	Generalizability to target population. Collect sufficient data for multivariate analyses that evaluate the relationships between multiple factors and outcomes of interest. Theory evaluation through hypothesis testing. Suitable for sensitive or controversial topics.	No insights from respondents. Can't be changed if the wrong questions are asked. Very few difficult questions can be asked. Difficult to establish causality unless using a panel survey or linking survey data to other sources.
Semi-structured questionnaire	In-depth insights. Interviewer can probe for more details.	Small scale due to high costs. Low generalizability. Not appropriate for closed questions. Limited options for multivariate analysis.
Case studies	In-depth insights. Provide ideas for theory development. Explore/identify causal factors.	Not generalizable to a population. Selected cases can be outliers that are not representative of the population. Often no comparison group.

Note: For an expanded list of advantages and disadvantages, see Nardi (2018, table 1.1).

analyses of survey data. Table 2.2 summarizes some of the main advantages and disadvantages of each method of gathering original data in respect to research questions.

Survey research questions can gather data to test hypotheses or remain exploratory if there is insufficient evidence from the literature to suggest the relationship between variables. If hypotheses are used, the survey questions must be written in a way that tests each hypothesis. This may require considerable thought on how to translate theoretical constructs into simple questions. A poorly written question may obtain data that does not test the hypothesis, creating an unacceptable temptation to change the interpretation of the question to fit the theory. Questions need to be interpreted exactly as written and as understood by respondents, so it is important to carefully write and test survey questions.

There are four general types of variables that can be produced using survey data: dependent variables that measure outcomes, independent variables that test hypotheses, control variables that do not test hypotheses but can affect the outcome of interest, and interaction or instrumental variables that mediate the effect of an independent variable on a dependent variable. Variables for analysis can be constructed from a single survey question or from multiple survey questions; for instance, a variable on the variety of innovations can be constructed by summing responses to five yes or no questions on specific types of innovations.

Answering research questions can require descriptive or multivariate analyses (Nardi, 2018). Descriptive analyses provide frequencies (what percentage of respondents did x) or correlations (what activities are associated with other variables). Frequencies require data from random samples of a population and either high response rates or adequate treatment of potential non-respondent bias to accurately represent the population of interest. Multivariate analyses such as regressions or structural equation modelling that evaluate relationships between different multiple variables also benefit from random samples and high response rates, but worthwhile data for regression can also be obtained from surveys with low response rates (Dassonneville et al., 2020).

There are two common mistakes in translating research questions into survey questions. The first is to fail to include in a questionnaire all questions that are needed to construct all necessary variables. The second mistake is to include questions that are not needed, since this will increase questionnaire length and reduce response rates (Chapter 3). This is often caused by designing a questionnaire to cover everything that might be of interest, instead of first identifying all necessary variables and resisting the temptation to add 'nice to know' questions (section 3.2).

Regrettably for overly enthusiastic researchers but a relief for respondents, there are limits on the types and number of questions that can be asked in a questionnaire, which needs to be easy to understand and require no more than 15 minutes to complete. Conceptually difficult questions can be asked in a semi-structured questionnaire but may be unsuitable for a structured questionnaire. Section 3.4.2 describes methods to reduce the difficulty of questions.

2.4   COMPATIBILITY BETWEEN RESEARCH QUESTIONS AND SURVEY CHARACTERISTICS

Ensuring that the survey questions can answer the research questions is only part of what needs to be considered. In addition, the questions need to be compatible with three characteristics of a survey: the target population and sampling method, the statistical models that will be used to analyse the collected data (which varies by the measurement level for questions), and the choice of survey method.

2.4.1   Target Population and Sample

Two characteristics of the target population and sample can influence the design of survey questions and vice versa: each potential respondent's area of expertise and the type of sample.

First, questionnaires need to be addressed to appropriate individuals who have the experience and knowledge to answer the questions. In a survey of organizations, this requires identifying the best type of potential respondent for a questionnaire, which can also influence the organizational unit to sample.

In statistical terms, each part of an organization that has some degree of decision-making power is called a 'unit' and can be the target of a survey. Organizations with more than 50 employees are often divided into divisions or establishments, each of which can be a unit of interest. Governments have separate ministries and agencies that can be further divided into departments and service-oriented establishments such as hospitals, universities and schools, which in turn can have separate divisions such as radiology and surgery departments in hospitals or faculties in universities. Businesses are divided into divisions, establishments ('kind of activity units') such as manufacturing plants, and subsidiaries in different geographical locations or industries.

With a few exceptions, respondents should only be asked to answer questions on topics for which they have personal experience and knowledge. This often requires directing respondents to only answer questions on their unit or area of responsibility. For example, the manager of a hospital radiology department could be asked to answer most questions in respect to the radiology department only. This would exclude all employees working in other units of the hospital, such as maintenance staff affiliated to a different unit, even though they may also be responsible for the maintenance of the radiology department. There are two exceptions to this rule: questions on other organizations where perceptions are important, such as the views of business managers on the level of competition from other firms, and questions on the practices or strategies of the larger organization of which the respondent's unit is a part, if there is a reasonable expectation, confirmed during questionnaire testing (Chapter 4), that respondents will know the answer. For instance, all managers should be aware of general organizational strategies or human resource practices governing staff conflicts such as bullying.

Second, many research questions require taking a probability or random sample of the population, such as questions that require frequency data or evaluating patterns in the distribution of variables. Most types of multivariate analyses require sufficiently large random samples to provide adequate statistical power to minimize Type II errors that occur when an incorrect null hypothesis is not rejected. In some cases, research questions that are focused on exploratory research can use smaller surveys that use non-random sampling methods (section 5.5.2).

2.4.2   Statistical Models and Measurement Level

Ensuring that the questionnaire matches the research questions also requires thinking about the statistical models that will be used to analyse the data and the measurement level for the dependent and independent variables (section 7.2). For instance, Ordinary Least Squares (OLS) assumes that data are normally distributed and requires interval level data for the dependent variable, such as the change in revenue in the previous year. Other models such as probit or logit models are appropriate for binary (yes or no) dependent variables, while ordered logit or probit models can be used to analyse ordinal dependent variables. Poisson models are suitable for dependent variables measured as count data, such as the number of patents. The use of principal component analysis (PCA) or other forms of factor analysis to reduce the number of independent variables may require ordinal level data.

2.4.3   Survey Method

Surveys can be implemented through 'heard' interview methods such as face-to-face and computer assisted telephone interviews (CATI) or by 'read' methods such as a printed questionnaire delivered to sampled individuals by post or online questionnaires. The choice of a 'heard' or 'read' method influences the topics that can be covered in a questionnaire and the question formats. Interview methods are more likely than read questionnaires to elicit socially desirable responses (Zhang et al., 2017) and should be avoided for what may be, depending on the culture, socially sensitive topics such as diversity or gender. Respondents are more likely to give accurate responses to sensitive questions in an online versus a CATI format (Huang, 2006; Lee et al., 2019). Conversely, a large number of open questions to examine perceptions, opinions and values are more suited to an interview format than read questionnaires (Fink, 2003). Matrix or grid questions that use ordinal response categories for multiple questions on a related topic (section 3.7.1) should be used sparingly in interview formats because they are tiresome for interviewees. A read survey format is preferable if the research questions require more than two or three matrix questions. An exception is when surveys are completed using a smartphone, where the screen may be too small to manage matrix questions.

2.5   RESPONSE RATES AND DATA QUALITY

Two types of response rates are relevant to a questionnaire survey. The most familiar is the survey response rate, or the number of individuals who completed and returned the questionnaire (the numerator) divided by the number who were sampled and received the questionnaire (the denominator). This response rate is frequently adjusted by subtracting from the denominator individuals who could not be located or who had left the target population, for instance if they had changed jobs or retired. The second type is the item response rate, calculated for returned questionnaires only, and equals the percentage of respondents that answer a question (or sub-question item in a matrix question) out of the total number of respondents who were eligible to answer the question. Eligibility can vary because of the use of filters in a questionnaire that direct respondents to different questions. For example, only managers in a business with a diversity programme would be eligible to answer a set of questions on the effects of the programme on employee well-being.

A major goal for surveys is to obtain a good survey response rate and good item response rates for all questions. The focus is usually on the survey response rate, but the item response rate is important for data quality and analysis. The survey response rate is affected by two factors: the average propensity of the target population to participate in a survey, which varies by country and culture, and the effort expended by the survey team to increase response rates by implementing good survey practices (Beullens et al., 2018).

Item response rates tend to decline for questions placed near the end of a long questionnaire and are lower for difficult questions, such as questions asking for interval level data such as a business's total revenue or profits in the previous year. The important implication is that a questionnaire should be as short as possible and contain very few difficult questions.

Low survey response rates create two problems. The first is that the number of returned questionnaires may be insufficient for the planned analyses, particularly when the goal is to compare phenomena among multiple groups, such as the use of specified business strategies by a sample of businesses in 20 sectors. A sufficient sample size is needed to detect statistically significant differences, with the size of the sample depending on the expected prevalence of business strategies in each sector (section 5.5.3).

The second problem is bias, which occurs when the characteristics of the respondents differ systematically from those of non-respondents in important ways that are correlated with variables of interest (Fulton, 2018; Hendra and Hall, 2019). A low response rate does not necessarily create bias, for instance if the reasons for non-response are randomly distributed between the respondents and non-respondents, but the probability of important differences in the data is expected to increase with low response rates. If your results are biased, you will not be able to provide descriptive results such as frequencies or claim that your results are representative of a population.

Low response rates are more prevalent for groups of individuals that are often the target of organizational surveys, such as executives (Anseel et al., 2010) and managers, versus supervisors or other employees (Mellahi and Harris, 2016). In addition, a review of published studies of surveys in management journals finds that the survey response rate declines as the topic of the questionnaire shifts from the individual, with an average 52.5% response rate, to a work team (average 47.0% response rate), and to the organization (average 39.2% response rate) (Mellahi and Harris, 2016). Plausible explanations for this decline is that respondents are reluctant to answer questions on their organization due to confidentiality concerns, or that survey topics that focus on the individual are more interesting to respondents. In respect to the latter, Fink (2003) argues that a survey should only be used when the researcher is positive that the sampled individuals will be interested in the topic.

Due to a well-documented decline in survey response rates over the past decades (Hiebl and Richter, 2018; Koen et al., 2018), several studies have evaluated the effect of low response rates on survey results and have found that low response rates are only weakly associated with non-respondent bias in a way that affects the results of analyses (Curtin et al., 2000, Groves, 2006; Groves and Peytcheva, 2008; Hendra and Hall, 2019; Kohut et al., 2004). Many of these studies have evaluated the effect of low response rates by comparing survey results for specific variables from early responders to a survey to the results from later responders. There is often no or only small differences in the value of the selected variables between early and later respondents. However, there were small, significant differences in one study for a compound variable for the characteristics of the respondents (Hendra and Hall, 2019). Another study that used the same method found statistically significant differences between early and late respondents by several organizational characteristics, including the organization's revenue and number of employees.

The conclusion that can be drawn from research on survey response rates is that low response rates are not necessarily a disaster, but it is better to have a higher response rate. This is particularly important for voluntary surveys where response rates over 60% are very difficult to obtain. Substantive effort needs to be put into voluntary surveys to obtain a response rate of 40%. If you are starting with a defined budget, you need to implement the best survey practice that you can afford. If you have not yet applied for research funding, request sufficient funding to cover good survey practices and justify the need for sufficient funding. If you need additional motivation to adopt practices to increase the response rate, the editors of peer-reviewed journals view a good

Table 2.3   Tasks influencing question reliability and validity

Measure	Definition	Relevant tasks
Question reliability	Questions elicit 'true' answers for each individual respondent; individuals who share similar characteristics will provide similar answers.	Cognitive testing
Question validity	Questions measure what they claim to measure, providing accurate results.	Cognitive testing
Content validity	Questions appropriately assesses a characteristic or phenomena (response options are suitable).	Cognitive testing
Face validity	Questionnaire includes all necessary questions and asks questions using appropriate language.	Theory translation; cognitive testing
Construct validity	Questions can distinguish between respondents who do and do not report similar events, strategies, etc.	Theory translation
Internal consistency	Selected question items assess the same underlying characteristic or phenomena.	Post-survey analysis (Cronbach's alpha); confirmatory factor analysis (CFA)

response rate as an important criterion in publication decisions (Beullens et al., 2018).

Both questionnaire design and the implementation method will affect the response rate. Therefore, you need to pay careful attention to both, following the good practices outlined in Chapters 3 and 4 for questionnaire development and Chapter 5 for survey implementation. Good response rates will also improve data quality. If you obtain a response rate less than 80% (which is very likely), you will need to conduct analyses to identify and evaluate differences between your respondents and non-respondents, as described in section 6.2.2.

2.5.1   Question Reliability and Validity

There are multiple measures of data reliability and questionnaire validity that can be affected by how theory is translated into questions and the process of developing and testing questions. Table 2.3 summarizes several measures of reliability and validity and the techniques that are required to get good results. Careful theory translation and cognitive testing (Chapter 4) play key roles in ensuring question reliability and validity.

2.6   BUDGET AND TIME REQUIRED

The budget for a survey is closely associated with the time required to under-take each stage of the survey process, so it is useful to estimate them together.

A budget is usually required as part of a research grant application, but if existing funds are available budget estimates are needed to determine which survey method is possible and the number of contacts that are affordable. The budget should cover the cost of (1) developing and cognitive testing the questionnaire, (2) survey implementation, which includes pre-survey preparation, constructing the sample and survey delivery, and (3) post-survey data entry and cleaning activities. The budget should also estimate (4) non-personnel costs such as material and travel costs. A separate time budget should estimate the time, in calendar months, to complete all survey tasks, from questionnaire development to data cleaning.

2.6.1   Questionnaire Development and Testing

The main cost for questionnaire development is the time of the people involved in this task. They may not require additional funding, but if part of a research grant proposal, allow approximately ten to 20 days to be shared between a minimum of two people. The number of days depends on experience with question design and familiarity with the topic. More time is required if it is necessary to carefully evaluate the literature to identify the types of questions that need to be included in the questionnaire. The number of required days will also increase if you are developing the questionnaire as part of a multi-centre research project because more people will be involved in suggesting, discussing and reviewing the questions. An additional budget for translation costs is required if the questionnaire will be implemented in two or more countries using different native languages, for example the United States and Germany.

Questionnaires must undergo face-to-face cognitive testing, as explained in Chapter 4, for a minimum of ten interviews. although it is better to aim for 30. Allow for approximately one day per completed interview, which includes time to identify and contact interviewees, time to prepare interview documents, two hours for the interview (two people for a one-hour interview), travel time for two people, time to summarize and assess the interview results, and time to send out thank-you emails to participants. Printing costs are negligible but do include a budget for travel costs to attend interviews.

2.6.2   Implementation

Implementation includes multiple activities discussed in Chapter 5, but before you can estimate a budget you will need to have selected your survey method (section 5.2) and estimated the minimum size of the realized sample required for your analyses, after adjusting for your expected response rate (section 5.5.3). Tasks that need separate budget lines include pre-survey preparation tasks, identifying your target population, selecting individuals to sample and obtaining contact details for them, and questionnaire delivery. The first two steps need to be done in-house, but questionnaire delivery, data compilation and identifying your sample can be contracted out to a professional survey company. Even if you plan to contract out part of the work, you should estimate a budget to ensure that you identify all necessary steps. The budget will also be useful for negotiating a contract with a survey company.

Pre-survey preparation

Several tasks need to be completed before the survey is ready to be launched into the field: obtaining ethics approval where necessary, writing a survey protocol, preparing different versions of the questionnaire (for instance an online version for a combined postal–online survey), preparing data entry forms for postal returns, and preparing an Excel file for tracking all returns during the survey delivery phase. Most of these tasks require between a half-day and two days. The time involved to prepare, submit and potentially revise an ethics approval request should take no longer than one day for a low-risk ethics approval and possibly two days for a high-risk approval (section 5.3.1). Estimate one to two days for writing the survey protocol, depending on your level of experience. Preparing a data entry form and an excel file for tracking returns should take less than half a day for each task.

Identifying your target population

This activity requires desk research to identify units of interest for your survey. The time required will vary substantially by the type of units that you need to identify and by the number of units. For instance, your target population might consist of all municipalities, secondary schools or universities in a defined region. This will not take much time since publicly available data are available for these organizations. Slightly more time will be required if you are interested in sub-units, such as municipal departments responsible for infrastructure or university faculties of archaeology. More time will be required if there are no publicly available data on your target population. For example, there are public data on manufacturing businesses, but such data may not exist for specific business characteristics of interest to you, such as businesses using robotics or open software. In these examples you will need to identify businesses that are likely to use robotics or open software, either based on their sector of activity or by searching corporate websites.

Sample selection and contact details

Sample selection requires collecting contact details for named individuals (section 5.6.1) and is time-consuming if there is no up-to-date list of potential contacts, requiring phone calls to collect contact details. In this case, allow 0.5 hours per contact. This can be a major survey cost. A goal to collect contact details for 1,200 individuals would require 75 person days. The task requires personable individuals who are comfortable with cold-calling and are able to obtain the necessary details from receptionists who are reluctant to provide this information. If there is an up-to-date list of potential contacts, for instance from government or corporate websites, allow 0.25 hours per contact.

Survey delivery

All survey methods will require staff time to prepare a first contact letter to be printed and mailed to sampled individuals and several reminder letters. The costs of distributing questionnaires depends on the choice of survey method.

The costs of a CATI survey include telephone calls, the software for data entry during the call, and interviewer time. Multiple interviewers are usually necessary to complete a CATI survey. The time includes reading the questionnaire aloud and contacting potential respondents. Between 15 and 30 minutes may be needed, with more time required if multiple calls are required to speak to the person. Allow additional time to conduct the interview and a short break for the interviewer between interviews. A 15-minute questionnaire interview could require an average of 20 minutes for the telephone contacts and five minutes for a break between interviews, totalling 40 minutes per respondent. If you expect a high rate of refusals to be interviewed, allow additional time to make multiple contacts per interview.

More time is required for a face-to-face survey for the same length of questionnaire because the interviewers need to introduce themselves and possibly answer questions. There are also additional costs for travel time and transport costs.

Online-only survey costs include the survey software provided by online survey companies such as Qualtrics or Survey Monkey, and ongoing costs of a staff person to manage the online survey and to reply to respondent questions. There are likely to be very few questions if the questionnaire is well designed and the cover letter is comprehensive. The initial contact letter for an online survey should be sent by post, which requires expenditures on printing and postage.

All survey methods require personnel time to maintain an up-to-date spreadsheet on contacts, completed questionnaires, follow-up reminders to non-respondents, and checking questionnaire returns for missing responses that may require a follow-up email or telephone call. Personnel costs for postal surveys include time to prepare mail-outs, such as filling envelopes, and data entry costs, either manually or for machine readable questionnaires. The number of hours required will depend on the number of contacts. The time for managing postal and online surveys will be highest at the start of the survey (allow half a day of employee time per day for the first month, dropping to one day per week in the last month).

Follow-up reminders are not relevant for CATI and face-to-face surveys, but do allow time for sending post or email reminders to non-respondents in postal and online surveys.

Small semi-structured interview surveys need to be done in-house, since they require highly motivated interviewers who are knowledgeable about the topic, but survey delivery for structured questionnaires can be contracted out. Professional survey companies may prefer to only use CATI or online survey methods because they are faster than a postal survey or a combined online/ postal survey. These companies are particularly advantageous for a CATI survey because they have trained individuals for making the initial contact and for conducting the interviews. You may need to budget time to explain the contents and purpose of the questionnaire to the interviewers so that they are prepared to answer interviewee questions during the survey.

Non-personnel costs
For a postal survey using a printed questionnaire, non-personnel costs include printing, extra postage for the additional weight of the printed survey in the first contact letter and in one of the follow-up reminders, and postage for two or more reminders. Other non-personnel costs include travel time for cognitive interviews and telephone costs.

Post-survey data collection
These costs include data cleaning and data entry. Data cleaning applies to all surveys but requires more care for postal surveys. Data are automatically entered into an electronic file for interview and online survey methods. Data entry costs can be substantial for printed questionnaires that are not machine readable. In addition to time savings, using machine readable questionnaires will reduce errors from manually entering results into a data file.

2.6.3   Budgetary Economies of Scale

The most practical way of looking at budgetary costs is in terms of cost per response. Some of these costs are fixed regardless of the number of responses, such as the cost of questionnaire development, cognitive testing, and writing the survey protocol, contact letter and reminder letters. Other budgetary costs for implementation include large economies of scale, where increasing the number of expected responses results in a less than proportionate increase in costs. The costs of doubling the number of expected responses to an online survey from 500 to 1,000, for example, may only incur a 20% increase in survey delivery costs (not including charges from online survey platforms such as Qualtrics). Other costs are proportionate to the number, with a doubling in the number of responses doubling the cost. Proportionate costs include identifying

Table 2.4   Timeline for a combined postal–online survey

Weeks from start date	Task	Task
0–2	Questionnaire development	Ethics approval
3–4		
5–6	Cognitive testing	Construct sample
7–8		
9–10	Pre-survey preparation	
11–12	Survey implementation including follow-up	
13–14		
15–16		Data entry for postal questionnaires
17–18		
19–20		
20–22		
23–24	Post-survey data cleaning	
24–26		

contact details, postage, time to prepare postal mail-outs, data entry for printed questionnaires, and coding or translating text fields in open questions.

2.6.4   Example of a Cost Budget

Table 2.4 provides an example of the calendar time to implement a combined postal and online survey of a sample of 1,000 managers that starts by post and switches to online after two reminders. With sufficient staff, it is possible to conduct several tasks at once, which reduces the total time required to 26 weeks. Work to construct the sample can be underway at the same time as cognitive testing and pre-survey preparation. Data entry for postal questionnaires should be concurrent with survey implementation, with the results of each returned questionnaire entered into the data file shortly after arrival. This also reduces the risk of misplacing returned questionnaires.

Table 2.5 provides an example of the budget for the survey in Table 2.4. The estimate is based on two junior staff and one senior staff member. The budget includes personnel time and non-personnel expenses. The cost of reminders needs to be estimated using expected response rates after each stage. In Table 2.5 a 10% response is expected after the first contact, reducing the number of necessary first reminder letters.

Table 2.5   *Budget estimate for a combined postal and online survey*

Task	Junior staff days	Senior staff days	Notes
Develop questionnaire		10	Multiple iterations expected
Cognitive testing			
Contact respondents, set up interviews	4		
Cognitive testing interviews phase 1	5	5	Approx. 20 interviews, 4 per day
Cognitive testing interviews phase 2	2.5	2.5	Approx. 10 interviews, 4 per day
Travel time	2	2	
Summarize results	3	3	
Discuss, revise and format questionnaire	1	1	
Pre-survey preparation			
Ethics approval (low risk)		1	
Write protocol		1	
Produce online version + testing	1	1.5	No costs for friends, etc., to test
Prepare data entry form for postal returns	0.5		
Produce Excel file for tracking returns	0.5		
Identifying target population and sample construction			
Identify population*	35	2	5,000 mid-level managers*
Draw random sample	0.5	0.25	1,000 managers
Sample selection and contact details	60	2	Desk research and phone calls
Survey implementation			
Mail-out of first contact	4	1	Envelope stuffing, etc.
First reminder mail-out	2		"
Second reminder with questionnaire	3		"
First contact online	0.5		
Online reminder email	0.5		
Tracking of responses	14	1	Over time survey is in the field
Post-survey data entry and cleaning			Expect 300 postal returns, 15
Data entry for printed questionnaires	10	1	minutes data entry apiece
Data cleaning	10		
Total personnel	159	34.25	
Daily cost including on-costs	400	800	
Total personnel costs	63,600	27,400	
Other costs	*Cost in euros*		
Questionnaire printing costs		2,500	1 per questionnaire, 2,500 copies
Postage contact letter + questionnaire		2,400	2.4 per package

Postage first reminder letter	900	1 per letter
Postage reminder letter + questionnaire	1,920	Expected 800 reminders
Travel costs for cognitive testing	500	Bus/train for two people
Total other costs	8,220	
Total personnel and other costs	99,220	

Note: * Budget assumes that some contact data are available on mid-level managers, such as from organograms.

2.7 CONCLUSIONS

An understanding of all tasks required for a questionnaire survey, and how different tasks are related, is necessary for translating research questions into survey questions and to select the survey method. Good practices, as outlined in Chapters 3, 4 and 5, need to be followed to obtain a good response rate and high-quality data. The survey method (CATI, face-to-face, postal or online) needs to be selected before estimating a calendar time budget and a financial budget, since the survey method has a substantial effect on both the timeline and costs.

3. Questionnaire design

3.1   INTRODUCTION

A well-designed questionnaire must meet many requirements. It needs to be interesting for respondents, able to be completed within 15 minutes or less, contain clearly written questions that can be understood as intended by all respondents, ensure that all respondents can provide reasonably accurate answers to all questions, minimize undesirable response behaviour, maximize survey and item response rates, avoid potential issues of common method bias, contain no more questions than needed nor omit any necessary questions to answer research questions, and use appropriate measurement levels for addressing the research questions. This is an extensive list that should convince you that designing and testing a questionnaire (an essential part of questionnaire design that is covered in Chapter 4) will take considerably longer than a few days or weeks. These requirements for a good questionnaire fall under six main topics: translating research questions into survey questions, questionnaire length, question design and content, question types, questionnaire layout, and delivery method.

The experts on the design of questions and questionnaire layout for surveys of organizations such as businesses, households, government agencies and non-profits are National Statistical Offices (NSOs). Some of the leaders in the field include the Australian Bureau of Statistics, Statistics Canada, INSEE in France, the Central Bureau of Statistics (CBS) Netherlands, Statistics Norway, Statistics Sweden, and the Office for National Statistics (ONS) for the United Kingdom. All of these NSOs (plus many others not listed here) have a history of careful evaluation of layouts and the use of cognitive testing (section 4.2) to test survey questions. Before starting to develop and format your questions, you should download business or other types of organizational or individual questionnaires of interest to you from your NSO and from one or more of the NSOs listed above. In addition to examples of good layout and question design practices, NSO questionnaires may include questions that you can adopt or adapt to your own needs. Unfortunately, it may take some searching online to find the questionnaire rather than a document providing the results of a survey. You may need to contact the NSO by email or telephone to obtain a link to a questionnaire. It will be well worth the effort. You should also look at academic surveys in your topic of interest, but make sure that the questions have been cognitively tested.

Do not, however, use NSO questionnaires as good examples of questionnaire length. NSO questionnaires are usually compulsory and therefore often excessively long and demanding, even running to 50 pages.

3.2   TRANSLATING RESEARCH QUESTIONS INTO SURVEY QUESTIONS

Unless you are preparing a survey that individuals will be required by law to complete (as with NSO surveys), your survey will be non-compulsory, with no legal compunction for people to answer. Unfortunately, response rates for non-compulsory surveys have been declining for decades (Fulton, 2018; Hiebl and Richter, 2018; Stedman et al., 2019). In this environment, you will need to make your questionnaire as short as possible, given a strong negative relationship between questionnaire length, or time to complete, and the questionnaire response rate (Best and Krueger, 2004; Bogen, 1996; Rolstad et al., 2011; Sahlqvist et al., 2011).

A common error that results in too many questions, or difficult or ambiguous questions that take too much time to answer, is a lack of thought on how to translate research questions and hypotheses into survey questions. Before starting a questionnaire, you need to carefully think through the data that you require and their measurement level (nominal, ordinal, interval or ratio). This exercise needs to draw on the existing literature of relevance to your research questions – do not start developing a questionnaire without a thorough review of the literature.

If you plan to test hypotheses, it is helpful at this point to draw up a table including all independent, interaction (modifier) and control variables that you expect to influence each of your dependent variables. Each variable should be fully described in writing, although the description does not need to be a draft version of the question. If you plan to conduct multivariate analyses, it is essential to collect data for more than one dependent variable, or, if you only have a single dependent variable in mind, alternative methods of measuring it. For example, if you plan to use a performance measure for your dependent variable, identify several relevant ways of measuring performance. This is because a single dependent variable from a questionnaire can fail, for instance if a high percentage of respondents did not answer the question, there is insufficient variation in the dependent variable, or if none of your independent variables has a significant effect on the value of your dependent variable.

The same requirement to think through your analyses also applies when the survey will only be able to collect exploratory data. This will occur if you can't generate testable hypotheses because of an insufficiently developed theory, due to very little or no existing research on your topic. In this case you may plan to focus on collecting descriptive data. Draw up tables of how you intend to present the data, including cross-tabulations of different variables of interest. These will help you to identify the variables you need to collect and subsequently the types of questions that you will need to write.

The purpose of these table-writing exercises is, first, to limit the number of questions you develop and, second, to make sure that you do not forget to collect data for what might be an important variable. The goal is to produce a questionnaire that collects all essential data but collects no data that you won't use. In practice this never happens. A few questions always slip in that end up being of little value, but you want to minimize this outcome.

A popular alternative to producing tables of independent and dependent variables is to draft an unlimited number of questions that *might* be of interest, with a plan to reduce the number at a later stage, for instance dropping 'nice to know' but not essential questions. This is poor practice because almost everyone finds it difficult to delete questions that they lovingly developed with great care and attention, so it is much more effective to not develop extraneous questions in the first place. However, a combination of producing tables and a slightly more generous acceptance of 'nice to know' questions might be necessary for exploratory research.

The length of a questionnaire can also be kept manageable if there are alternative sources of data that can be linked to your respondents. For example, you should be able to collect data on the function of an organizational unit and the job title of the unit's manager from publicly available data such as organograms posted on organizational websites. You may also need this data to construct your sample (section 5.5). Relevant data on the number of employees in a business are often available on company websites or data can be purchased from data compilers such as Dun and Bradstreet in the United States and other countries. In Europe, the Amadeus or Orbis database maintained by Bureau van Dijk provides data on employment, sector and finance for over 500,000 public and private companies in 43 European countries, while Orbis also provides data for other countries. These databases are searchable by industry classes, size and other characteristics. Many universities subscribe to these databases and provide free access for research staff.

3.2.1   Extra Survey Question to Address Open Data Requirements

There is a global movement to make microdata collected through publicly funded studies available to other researchers. If this is applicable to you, you may need to include a question at the end of your questionnaire that asks respondents if they agree to providing their results to academics outside your study group (section 5.3). Due to confidentiality requirements, you can't share the original microdata, but it is possible to share microdata that has been anonymized by removing all information that could be used to identify the respondent or the respondent's organization. Two methods for anonymization are described in section 6.3.3.

3.3   QUESTIONNAIRE LENGTH

Length can be measured in the time required to complete the questionnaire or the number of question items (Best and Krueger, 2004). Both are more important than page length, although the number of pages will influence potential respondents' perceptions of the length of a printed questionnaire. A non-compulsory questionnaire should not take more than 15 minutes for most respondents to complete and average completion times of ten minutes will be better. Questionnaires that will be answered on a smartphone should not take more than ten minutes.

A printed questionnaire should be fewer than ten pages in length, including a cover page with no questions and space at the end for written comments. Do not attempt to reduce the page length by compressing the text. Each page of a printed or online questionnaire needs to contain ample 'white' space – areas with no text. The first half of Table 3.1 gives an example of two questions that lack sufficient white space, while the second half of Table 3.1 gives an example of adequate white space for the same questions. The layout of the questionnaire will also affect perceptions of the length and time to reply, such as the font, use of colours, contrast between the text and the background, etc. Section 3.6 covers layout in more detail.

The time required to complete a questionnaire is influenced not only by the number of questions, but by the time required for respondents to answer each question. Difficult questions require more time to answer. Three aspects of a question will increase its difficulty: the effort required to understand the content of a question and how to answer it, asking about events that occurred more than a few months in the past, and asking for numeric data, such as expenditures on specific activities or the percentage of staff with specific characteristics (highest level of educational attainment, etc.) or responsibilities.

3.4   QUESTION CONTENT AND DESIGN

The content of each question concerns the meaning of the question, the time period covered and the type of data that it collects. The content of the questionnaire influences respondent interest and is, of course, the key purpose of your questionnaire. The design of a question includes vocabulary and syntax, definitions and filters. Question design affects respondent comprehension, the

Table 3.1   Questions with insufficient and sufficient white space

1. Insufficient white space
1. In 2022, was your office responsible for some or all of the patenting, licensing or other knowledge transfer activities of a: *(Check all that apply.)*
☐   General university (both humanities and sciences)
☐   Technical university (mostly science and technology)
☐   Hospital (linked to a university or independent)
☐   Government or non-profit research institute
☐   Research park or incubator affiliated with a university, hospital or research institute
☐   None of the above *(go to question 11)*
2. In 2022, was your office responsible for all patenting and licensing by the institution(s) checked in question 1? *(Hereafter referred to as 'your institution'.)*
☐   Yes *(go to question 3)*
☐   No Approximately what percentage of all patent applications by your institution was handled by your office in 2022?   _____%
2. Sufficient white space
1. In 2022, was your office responsible for some or all of the patenting, licensing or other technology transfer activities of a:
☐   General university (both humanities and sciences)
☐   Technical university (mostly science and technology)
☐   Hospital (linked to a university or independent)
☐   Government or non-profit research institute
☐   Research park or incubator affiliated with a university, hospital or research institute
☐   None of the above *(go to question 11)*
2. In 2022, was your office responsible for all patenting and licensing by the institution(s) checked in question 1? *(Hereafter referred to as 'your institution'.)*
☐   Yes *(go to question 3)*
☐   No Approximately what percentage of all patent applications by your institution was handled by your office in 2022?   _____%

accuracy of their responses and question difficulty. Both question content and design influence survey and item response rates.

3.4.1   Questionnaire Content

One of the most important factors influencing the survey response rate is respondent interest in the questions. A basic condition influencing interest is that respondents must perceive that the topic of the survey and the specific questions are relevant to them. A survey of marketing activities, for instance, is unlikely to be of high interest to human resource managers because they may not perceive that it is relevant to their work.

As a first step, building respondent interest requires a good contact letter that explains the purpose of the questionnaire (section 5.2). In addition, the questions must cover topics that are relevant to all surveyed individuals, including those that have no or limited experience with the topic. As an example, a survey on the innovation activities of public sector agencies should be designed to include questions of relevance to agencies that did not innovate. Otherwise, sampled individuals from agencies with no innovations could be less likely to complete the questionnaire than individuals from innovative agencies. This will create biased responses, particularly for univariate estimates such as the percentage of agencies with innovation activities.

Second, the questionnaire must include questions that are interesting, for example because they are novel, covering activities that respondents have not been asked about before; inspire reflection or awareness (it may not have occurred to human resource managers that personnel skills could be an important part of marketing their businesses' capabilities); or ask for the respondents' perceptions on important issues to them. A few questions on the respondents themselves may also be perceived as interesting, but it may be necessary for ethical or confidentiality reasons (section 5.3.2) to limit personal questions to non-sensitive subjects such as the number of years they have been in their current position, past work history or their highest level of education. Unavoidably, questionnaires will need to include several questions of low interest to respondents, but these should be kept to a minimum.

Time (reference period)

The reference period is the specified time period covered by a survey, for example the previous six months, previous year or a specific day, such as a question that asks about the number of employees at the end of the financial year. Defining a reference period is essential for sporadic activities, with the length of the reference period influencing the results. Questions with a reference period of several months or a year should obtain a positive response if an activity of interest occurred at any time within the reference period. For example, the question 'In the last year, did your business invest in artificial intelligence software systems' should be answered with a 'yes' if investment occurred on one day of the previous year. A one-year reference period should also obtain 'yes' responses for questions on activities that occurred for a few weeks or months within the reference period, such as a marketing campaign or a seasonal service provided to individuals.

To minimize problems with memory recall, the reference period should be no longer than six months to one year before the implementation of the questionnaire. However, a longer observation period may be needed for some research questions. For instance, OECD/Eurostat (2018) recommends that surveys of innovation should cover no less than the previous year and no more than three years. More than one reference period can be used in a question-naire, but it is best to use as few as possible.

3.4.2 Question Design

Vocabulary and syntax
The vocabulary and question structure influence respondent comprehension. Data quality will decline if respondents don't understand a question due to the use of jargon or complex syntax. This can result in incorrect answers. It is infrequent for respondents to deliberately give incorrect answers except for sensitive or controversial questions or questions that are affected by social desirability bias (Sjöström and Holst, 2002; Tourangeau and Yan, 2007). These types of questions should be rare in a survey of organizations. Problems can occur when respondents try to be helpful by answering a question that they don't understand. This can produce false positives due to a tendency for respondents to give positive answers (Schaeffer and Presser, 2003). To attain high data quality, questions need to be carefully written to maximize compre-hension and minimize incorrect answers.

The reading level, sentence structure and vocabulary of a questionnaire must optimize understanding for all respondents. This includes respondents who have a below average vocabulary, who are not native speakers of the language used in the questionnaire, and respondents who read questions very quickly. All respondents should not need to carefully ponder or think through a ques-tion to understand it. To meet these goals, sentences should be short, preferably no longer than 20 words, the reading level should be equivalent to the last year or two of high school (even when most respondents are likely to have a tertiary education), and the vocabulary used in the questionnaire should consist of widely understood words, avoiding specialized jargon or technical terms.

You should be particularly careful to avoid words that seem common to you because you and your colleagues use them frequently in your research, but that comprise specialized vocabulary that many of your respondents may

Table 3.2   *Avoiding the use of the unfamiliar terms by defining relevant*
                  actions

1. Did your work unit obtain ideas for better services through involving service users in co-creation activities?	
Yes	☐
No	☐
Don't Know	☐

Better alternative:

2. Did your work unit obtain ideas for better services through involving service users in the following activities?

	Yes	No	Don't know
a) One-to-one conversations to identify challenges or unmet needs	☐	☐	☐
b) Focus groups to identify challenges or unmet needs	☐	☐	☐
c) Brainstorming or idea generation workshops	☐	☐	☐
d) Observing how users experience or use a prototype of a service	☐	☐	☐

not understand. For example, a survey of public sector managers should not use terms such as tacit knowledge, co-creation, design thinking or governance. Some respondents will correctly understand these terms, but to minimize error all respondents must understand all vocabulary in your questionnaire. Furthermore, some terms such as 'co-creation' have different definitions, depending on the academic discipline or context. Instead of using a term such as 'co-creation', use common vocabulary to describe the activities that make up co-creation. This may require separate questions or response options for each activity, as shown in Table 3.2. Question 1 uses the term 'co-creation' and should not be used, while Question 2 asks about separate activities that are part of co-creation.

It is essential that questions are not ambiguous and open to different interpretations. Ambiguity can occur because of poorly thought-out research questions – the researcher is not entirely clear about what the question should ask – or because the question length has been shortened to save space. (Table 3.4 includes an ambiguous question that could have been due to poorly thought-out research questions). Although it is important for questions to be short, this must not occur at the expense of comprehension. Conversely, list and matrix questions (section 3.5 below) should not overlap by asking slightly different versions of the same concept or activity.

Table 3.3   *Example of a filter question*

1. In the last two years, did your firm introduce any of the following:		
	Yes	No
A new or improved good	☐	☐
A new or improved service	☐	☐
A new or improved method for producing goods or services	☐	☐
A new or improved method for delivering goods or services to your clients	☐	☐
If yes to any of the above, please go to question 6, otherwise go to question 11.		

Definitions

Respondents rarely look up definitions and therefore they should not be included in a glossary at the end of a printed questionnaire or in dropdown menus in an online questionnaire. Instead, definitions need to occur immediately after a question or preferably written into the question. If a definition refers to specific activities, as in the example in Table 3.2 for co-creation, include definitions in questions that also collect useful data.

'Don't know' response options

Providing a 'don't know' or 'not relevant/not applicable' response option will result in a shift in responses to these options from a 'low importance' or 'no' response category. In analysis, it may be possible to combine the 'don't know' or 'not relevant' responses with a 'no' response on the grounds that an activity was unlikely or of very low importance if the respondent does not know the answer. However, respondents can be frustrated by the lack of a 'don't know' or 'not relevant' option, leading to annoyance that results in skipping one or more questions. Therefore, it may be beneficial to include a 'don't know' option when you expect a non-trivial share of respondents to not know the answer. The 'don't know' response option can be excluded when all or almost all respondents are expected to know the answer. For example, all managers should be able to answer questions on the main functions of their work unit or the approximate number of staff in their work unit.

Filter questions and skip instructions

Filter questions obtain information for directing respondents to specific subsequent questions using skip instructions. This is often referred to as the 'branch logic' of a questionnaire. In the example in Table 3.3, the skip instructions below the question direct respondents who selected 'yes' to any of the four sub-questions to go to the following question 6, while respondents who answer 'no' to all four sub-questions are directed to go to question 11, skipping questions six to ten inclusive.

Table 3.4   *Example of a complex question*

Did your university department:	Yes	No
Establish a proactive strategy of open exchange (open dialogue with other stakeholders to narrow the gap between theory and the practice of higher education institutes) to support third mission activities?	☐	☐

The disadvantage of skip routines is that they can result in a loss of data if questions that would have been answered if seen (as in a printed questionnaire) are automatically skipped in online or interview surveys. In addition, using skip routines results in missing data for some respondents, which may create problems for some types of multivariate analysis that need all respondents to answer all questions to avoid self-selection issues. If this applies to your analysis, minimize the use of skip routines by writing questions that all respondents can answer, even if their response is 'no'.

Complex questions

Complex questions contain several phrases, often separated by commas, that require several conditions to occur simultaneously or sequentially. Complex questions are common in first drafts of questionnaires (and far too often in finished questionnaires) and need to be rewritten. Table 3.4 includes an example of an egregiously complex question in a survey of university professors.

The question is very difficult because of the long section in parentheses, but even without this section the question is poorly designed because it requires two conditions (a proactive strategy and open exchange) to be met for the core activity of a strategy to support third mission activities. This can be confusing for respondents, with the question unlikely to be understood quickly. The number of requirements increases if we add the material in parentheses: the strategy must be proactive, include open exchange with stakeholders, and the exchange must be oriented to narrowing the gap between theory and practice. Aside from its level of difficulty, which will create errors on its own, this question is seriously flawed because it could attract a high percentage of incorrect responses, notably from respondents who give a 'yes' response because they meet one or two of the conditions, when their correct answer should be 'no' because they do not meet all of them. Based on the question, the answer should only be 'yes' if all three requirements are met.

This question needs to be taken apart and rewritten as several questions, although this requires more details to describe what is meant by 'proactive' and by 'the gap between theory and practice'.

Table 3.5   *Example of questions that contain more than one question*

Does your university:	Yes	No
Conduct research on survey design that was presented at conferences?	☐	☐
Promote entrepreneurial principles and an innovation culture throughout the curriculum?	☐	☐
Define international top-level education and high attractiveness for students (international student mobility) as its mission?	☐	☐

Table 3.6   *Revision of question 2 in Table 3.5*

In [year] did your university department:	Yes	No
Promote entrepreneurial principles in one or more courses of your curriculum?	☐	☐
Promote an innovation culture in one or more courses of your curriculum?	☐	☐

Questions containing more than one question

Avoid questions that contain two or more sub-questions. They can often, but not always, be identified by the use of 'and' between two statements or activities. If you are asking about two related activities and are not interested in collecting separate data for each of them, use 'or' instead of 'and'.

Table 3.5 provides three examples of questions that include more than one question. The first example does not use 'and' but requires survey research to be presented at conferences. This is a limiting condition that will prevent the researcher from obtaining information on survey research that was made public using other methods. The second example includes 'and', 'promote entrepreneurial principles *and* an innovation culture', then refers to a condition that acts as a third question: these activities must occur 'throughout the curriculum'. The third question covers international top-level education *and* high attractiveness for students, then muddies understanding by the information in parentheses (international student mobility), which implies that the first two conditions are the definition of international student mobility.

Multiple questions within the same question create problems for respondents on how to answer. Using the second example in Table 3.5, what if an innovation culture is strongly promoted but not entrepreneurial principles? What if both entrepreneurial principles and an innovation culture are promoted but only in one compulsory course? The respondents will be left guessing as to what is expected of them, which will create undesirable differences in how respondents answer the question.

Questions which contain two or more questions need to be redesigned, which can require the use of filter questions that exclude respondents who do not meet the criteria to answer a subsequent question. The second question in Table 3.5 can be corrected by creating two separate questions on whether any courses promote entrepreneurial principles or an innovation culture, as shown in Table 3.6. The answers to these two questions can then be used as a filter for additional questions on the prevalence of these two activities in the curriculum.

Biased or leading questions

Questions can bias respondents if they use adjectives with desirable or undesirable connotations, such as 'concerned', 'enhanced', 'satisfied', etc. These terms can nudge respondents towards more negative or positive results. For example, the question 'Is senior management concerned about a lack of employee motivation?' could nudge the respondent to give a more critical appraisal than a neutral question, such as 'What is the level of employee motivation in your department?'

Appropriate response options

The response options for closed questions must be appropriate for the respondent (i.e. must logically and grammatically follow the question) and collect the required data for analysis. For example, don't provide an importance scale when a question refers to how common an activity is – this requires a frequency scale. Carefully check matrix questions for items that require a different response option than the one provided. It may be necessary to create two matrix questions or revise question items. Response options should also be simple and use no more than three to five words. 'Too early to estimate' is about as long as a response option can be. If you are using a sentence for a response option, turn the sentence into a question.

3.5   QUESTION TYPES

Questions can contain a single main question, a main question followed by a set of sub-questions (items), and different types of response options. The type of question varies by the measurement level for collecting data, which can be nominal, ordinal or numeric. Five question formats are commonly used: check lists and yes/no questions collect nominal data, ordinal and matrix or grid questions collect ordinal data, and numeric level questions collect interval, count or percentage data. A sixth question type is the open question, which collects qualitative data that can be recoded after the survey into nominal data. In many cases, data for a specific topic can be collected using nominal, ordinal or numeric questions. The decision on which measurement level to use depends on two conditions: the measurement level required by the statistical method for testing hypotheses (section 7.3) and the need to reduce the difficulty of the questionnaire.

Table 3.7   Example of a check list format for 'yes' responses

In the last two years, did your government work unit provide any of the following types of services?	
	(Tick all that apply)
1) Education services	☐
2) Health services	☐
3) Social welfare services	☐
4) Services to businesses	☐
5) Housing services	☐
6) Infrastructure services	☐
7) Services to other government units	☐
8) Other services	☐

3.5.1   Check List and 'Yes/No' (Dichotomous) Questions

Check lists and yes/no formats collect nominal data on the frequency of 'yes' responses for multiple items, as shown in Tables 3.7 and 3.8. The format for a check list includes a main question plus a series of items (Table 3.7), whereas the 'yes/no' format can include only a single main question or a main question and a list of items, as in Table 3.8. The check list assumes a 'no' response if an item is not selected.

The advantage of a check list is that it is easier for respondents to fill in, but it has an important disadvantage in that a blank can mean 'no' or it could mean that the respondent did not provide a response, with the question item unanswered and the data missing. Providing both a 'yes' and a 'no' option as in Table 3.8 permits the identification of missed items where neither the 'yes' nor 'no' response was checked. The 'yes/no' format can be extended to include a 'don't know' response option.

A major disadvantage of a check list as in Table 3.7 occurs when none of the items is selected. When this occurs, you won't know if the entire question was skipped or if the respondent considered all items and found that none of them warranted a 'yes' response. For this reason, only use check lists if you are reasonably confident that one or more of the items will be relevant to all respondents and that all possible options have been listed. In addition, just in case you have not included all possible options, include an 'other' option as in the example in Table 3.7 or a 'none of the above' option as the last item. Either of these two options should ensure that at least one item should be checked. If none of the question items is checked, assume that the entire question was not answered. It is also useful to add an instruction and space for the respondent to briefly describe what they had in mind if they checked 'other'. This information can often be recoded to one of the existing categories.

Table 3.8   Example of a 'yes/no' format

In the last two years, did your government work unit provide any of the following types of services?		
	Yes	No
1) Education services	☐	☐
2) Health services	☐	☐
3) Social welfare services	☐	☐
4) Services to businesses	☐	☐
5) Housing services	☐	☐
6) Infrastructure services	☐	☐
7) Services to other government units	☐	☐
8) Other services	☐	☐

Table 3.9   Example of an ordinal question

In the last two years, what percentage of your unit's employees received in-house training to improve their skills?	
	(Tick one box only)
a) None	☐
b) Less than 25%	☐
c) 25% to less than 50%	☐
d) 50% to less than 75%	☐
e) 75% or more	☐
f) Don't know	☐

A check list should not exceed nine items as respondents will be less likely to answer items placed later in the list. As relevant, respondents can be directed to check all items that apply to them, or to check only one, for instance the most relevant or most important option. Another variant of a nominal question is one that lists more than two categories of items for which only one response is possible. An example is a question on the country where the head office of a business is located.

3.5.2   Ordinal Questions

Ordinal level questions rank response categories along a scale that can be latent (for example 'importance') or clearly defined. Table 3.9 provides an example of an ordinal question where the response categories are defined and arranged in logical order, in this case the percentage of employees taking part in a specific activity. The question uses a single main question for which there are six mutually exclusive response categories, such that only one option is

Table 3.10   Matrix question

In the last two years, how important were the following factors in hindering or delaying the development of your unit's new or improved services?

(Tick one box per row)

	High	Medium	Low	None	Not relevant
Difficulty in obtaining funding to cover development costs	☐	☐	☐	☐	☐
Concerns over risk (failure of the innovation, negative publicity, technical difficulties, etc.)	☐	☐	☐	☐	☐
Lack of knowledge on how to develop new or improved services within your organization	☐	☐	☐	☐	☐
Resistance to change within your organization or by your stakeholders	☐	☐	☐	☐	☐
Opposition from other organizations that provide similar services	☐	☐	☐	☐	☐
Political or regulatory obstacles	☐	☐	☐	☐	☐
Other (please describe)	☐	☐	☐	☐	☐

valid. For ordinal questions with only one valid response, respondents must be directed to only check one item.

Other ordinal response options include count data, such as the number of employees in the respondent's unit (for instance nine or less, 10 to 24, 25 to 49, 50 to 249, 250 or more), financial data, such as the amount spent on an activity (less than $1,000, $1,000 to less than $10,000, $10,000 to less than $50,000, etc.) or frequency of an action (daily, at least once a week, several times per month, etc.). 'Likert' scales based on personal perceptions are commonly used, such as for importance (not important, slightly important, moderately important, very important) or agreement (strongly agree, agree, neutral, disagree, strongly disagree).

Matrix or grid questions include multiple items measured on an ordinal scale. They are commonly used to obtain respondent perceptions of the importance of multiple related factors. In the example given in Table 3.10, the related factors are obstacles to the development of a new or improved service. The response options can include anything measured on an ordinal scale, such as frequency or importance, but matrix questions are not advised for more demanding count or financial data, except for a very short list of items. To reduce satisficing behaviour (section 3.8), the number of question items in a matrix in all delivery formats (printed, online, face-to-face and CATI) should be limited to no more than nine question items and preferably fewer (Grady et al., 2019).

When an importance scale is used, the responses to items in a matrix question may be slightly correlated (interitem correlation) because of the question structure that lists multiple items one after the other (Couper et al., 2013). Respondents can see all question items, which will influence their answers to each item. For instance, the most important item to a respondent is very likely to influence their rating of the importance of other items in the question. This can be an advantage, as it ensures that the respondent uses the same interpretation of a latent scale for each question item.

3.5.3   Numerical Questions

Numerical data include interval, count and percentage data that have equal distances between all adjacent values, for instance the difference between 1% and 2% is identical to the difference between 56% and 57%. Examples include the number of employees in the work unit, the work unit's budget, or the percentage of employees that use each of several transportation modes (walking, bicycle, public transit, private car) to travel to work. Numerical level questions are difficult for respondents because they may require looking up the data in a file or giving careful thought to arrive at an answer. Numerical questions that ask for percentages can be particularly challenging because the respondent must estimate or know the total number involved (employees, budget, etc.), how the total is divided into different percentage categories and how to calculate a percentage (not everyone does).

Respondents to non-compulsory surveys are unlikely to look up numerical data. Instead, they frequently make educated guesses and round off their answers. Respondents to a question on the percentage of employees that received training are likely to round off to units of five (5%, 10%, 15%, etc.) or ten (10%, 20%, etc.) instead of reporting exact percentages such as 7% or 11%. Consequently, using an ordinal question with several response categories, as in Table 3.9, will be much easier for the respondent at a cost of only a minor loss of information.

Very few numeric questions should be included in a questionnaire, due to their high level of difficulty. Where possible, replace a numeric question with an ordinal question, as in Table 3.9. The most difficult question type asks for interval level data in the past, for instance the number of employees, total sales, or different types of expenditures two or more years ago. These types of questions are likely to have high item non-response rates that exceed 40% or 50%. If you must ask for interval data in the past, try to limit your questions to only one or two types of data and be prepared for a high share of missing responses.

When it is necessary to collect precise numerical data such as percentages, counts or expenditures, identify the expected units (thousands, millions, billions) and include instructions if rounding off is acceptable, such as to the nearest thousand or million currency units. The last three spaces in a response line or box for interval data include pre-filled with zeros to indicate rounding off to the nearest thousand currency units. Provide enough space for expected answers, for instance a box or line for total expenditures may need to allow for expenditures in billions or millions of currency units. Questions on calendar dates should indicate if data should be for the year and month or only the year (Couper et al., 2011).

3.5.4   Open Questions

Open questions do not provide the respondent with a defined response option (yes or no, ordinal scale, etc.) but ask the respondent to provide an answer in their own words. An example is a question asking the respondent to describe, in a few sentences, the most important challenge that their work unit faced in the previous year. Open questions are demanding of the respondent, but they are not as difficult as many interval level questions. Sufficient space should be provided for handwritten responses on printed questionnaires or for typed responses on online forms. The size of the space should approximate the length of the expected answer (Couper et al., 2011). Don't provide only one line or half a page if you expect two or three sentences. Open questions can also receive a high share of non-responses.

Open questions also require additional work for researchers to read handwriting (if using a printed questionnaire), for translation if the questionnaire is provided in several languages, and to code the results into easily manipulated data. An open question on the most important challenge faced by the respondent's work unit in the previous year could be coded by the type of challenge (insufficient employee skills, reorganization, etc.) and by the cause of the challenge (lack of funding, high employee turnover, etc.). A basic coding system for open questions should be generated during the translation of research questions into survey questions.

3.5.5   Changing the Measurement Level to Reduce Response Burden

The difficulty of a question and hence its respondent burden is lowest for yes/ no questions, intermediate for ordinal questions, and highest for numeric and open questions. Higher difficulty questions should only be used when they are necessary for the analytical methods that will be used to answer research questions. For example, if you plan to use principal component analysis (PCA) you might wish to include several ordinal matrix questions, or a planned dependent variable might require an interval level question. Nevertheless, many questions can be asked at a lower measurement level. An interval question for a dependent variable can be asked as an ordinal question, with the statistical regression model using an ordered probit or logit model instead of Ordinary Least Squares (OLS) (section 7.3). A question to collect ordinal data for an independent variable can be changed to a yes/no question that collects nominal data.

The choice of measurement level needs to be based on expectations for the distribution of responses. A yes/no question will be a poor measure of differences between respondents if 80% or more answer 'yes'. Instead, an ordinal question using an importance or frequency scale will be more useful. Questionnaire testing (Chapter 4) can identify the appropriate measurement level and the boundaries between categorical response options in an ordinal question.

3.5.6   Common Methods Bias

A potentially important issue that relates to the measurement level and the type of questions used in a questionnaire is the need to avoid common methods bias (or common variance bias), whereby statistically significant correlations between questions are artefacts of the questionnaire design, instead of a true correlation. Common method bias can potentially occur when almost all data for analysis are collected from the same source (such as one questionnaire) using the same question type, such as ordinal Likert questions (Tehseen et al., 2017). Concerns over common method bias are likely to be overstated, with several studies providing strong evidence that common methods bias is unlikely to be an issue for questionnaire research (Fuller et al., 2016; George and Pandey, 2017). Nevertheless, it is good practice to include nominal and ordinal questions and to use different response options for ordinal questions. Other techniques to reduce common methods bias are cognitive testing to ensure that your questions measure what is intended (Chapter 4), offering confidentiality to improve the honesty of responses (section 5.3.2) and, if possible, linking data from other sources to your survey results (section 6.3.1). There are post-survey statistical methods for detecting common method bias, as discussed in section 7.2.3.

3.6   QUESTIONNAIRE LAYOUT

The questionnaire layout (or format) includes all factors that influence the presentation of questions in printed and online (web) questionnaires, including correct alignment of response categories across questions and logical question order. Care needs to be taken with multimodal questionnaires that are read by respondents because the layout may need to differ between printed questionnaires and questionnaires delivered online to devices such as a desktop computer, laptop, tablet or smartphone.

The paragraph width for questions for printed questionnaires and for desktops and laptops should be short, for example taking up only the left-hand side of a page, while the response options can cross a larger fraction of the page. For both printed and all online devices, each page needs to contain a lot of white space (blank space with no text) and ample line spacing to avoid a crowded appearance. The contrast between text and the background should be crisp. Black on white has the highest contrast, but online contrast software can be used to ensure adequate contrast with a light coloured background. Do not use white or light coloured text on a dark background. Avoid complexity in the layout, such as multi-coloured backgrounds and multiple fonts that distract the respondent.

Fonts should be a minimum 11 point size for response options and larger for the main question in a matrix. Serif fonts will improve readability if there is a lot of text.

Good layout practices can vary by cultural preferences. Large fonts and a generous amount of white space on a page are needed for questionnaires in Europe, North America, Australia and New Zealand to create a relaxed environment for respondents. Conversely, in Japan and China questionnaires may use small fonts and exploit all available space on a page. You can find out what works best by checking the layout of recent questionnaires used by national statistical offices in the country or countries that you plan to survey.

3.6.1   Question Order and Placement

The order of questions in a questionnaire can influence answers. This can be helpful, for instance if an early question provides definitions or primes the respondent to think about activities that are returned to later in the questionnaire. Conversely, question order can be harmful if an early question biases responses to later questions.

Question order can also influence the response rate. Other than a small number of questions on the respondent, such as their work history or experience in their current position (Converse and Presser, 1986), questions in the early part of the questionnaire should be of high interest to the respondent, while more mundane questions should be included near or at the end of the questionnaire. It is not always possible to follow this guidance, as it may be necessary to first provide basic questions that are used in skip routines to direct the respondent to different parts of a questionnaire, or the initial questions may ask for basic information to ensure that the respondent's memory is primed for follow-on questions. For example, a survey on innovation will need to ask a question on whether the respondent's unit had innovated before asking questions that are more interesting to respondents.

3.7   DELIVERY METHOD

There are two main methods for delivering questionnaires. The first consists of printed and online (web) questionnaires that respondents read. The second consists of questionnaires that respondents hear in face-to-face interviews or telephone interviews. Both types of heard questionnaires use software that the interviewer uses to collect the responses, such as a form on a tablet used by a face-to-face interviewer or a computer assisted telephone interface (CATI) for a telephone interview. Both have the advantage of directly entering the responses into a data file that can be read by statistical software packages. Web-based methods for read questionnaires also automatically enter responses into a data file, but printed questionnaires need to be entered into a data file, either manually or using machine readable questionnaires.

The format of printed and online questionnaires, though both read, can be identical or differ due to options that are available for an online format that are not possible on a printed questionnaire, such as automated skip routines (branch logic), automatic reminders for skipped questions, or dropdown menus. Skip routines or branching instructions in a printed questionnaire should not be placed at the bottom of a page where respondents might miss seeing them (Belfo and Sousa, 2011). This is not an issue with online questionnaires as the skip routines are automated, with the next question seen by respondents based on their previous answers. Software for heard questionnaires can also automate skip routines and remind an interviewer if they accidentally skipped a question.

Differences between heard and read delivery methods may affect how respondents answer questions that can be due to the use of an interviewer versus reading a questionnaire or to differences in the cognitive processing of heard and read questions. Respondents to telephone interviews are more likely to provide extreme scores to Likert questions (for instance telephone formats elicit more 'not important at all' or 'extremely important' responses) than respondents to mailed or online formats (Dillman et al., 2009) while mailed or online formats are less subject to socially desirable responses (Lee et al., 2019). However, research that requires respondents to rank preferences finds few differences between data collected in a face-to-face interview versus an online questionnaire (Saloniki et al., 2019).

The use of two delivery methods can increase the survey response rate (section 5.2). Differences between heard and read questionnaires (section 2.4.3) suggest using two heard formats or two read formats, but common practice for a CATI survey is to provide a second option of a printed or online questionnaire because of the high cost of face-to-face interviews, even though this can reduce comparability. There are few differences in how respondents answer questions in online surveys completed on a desktop or laptop and mailed surveys if the layouts are similar, but the use of smartphones to answer questions can reduce comparability (section 3.7.2). If two delivery methods are used, care must be taken to make each version as similar as possible, which requires the questionnaire to be 'translated' from one format to another (Fink, 2003). An example of translation is given in Tables 3.11 and 3.12 for a read and heard matrix question.

3.7.1   Heard Questions: CATI and Face-to-Face Interview Questionnaires

Interview delivery methods suffer from two disadvantages. They are expensive due to the need for trained interviewers who are paid for the time of the interview plus travel time when the interviews are conducted face-to-face, and there are three important limitations to heard questionnaires that must be kept in mind when developing the questionnaire.

First, everything must be read by the interviewer, so the language needs to be designed to be heard instead of read. This requires the interviewer to read aloud both the instructions and the questions.

Second, interval level questions that require the respondent to think about the answer or look up data are less suited to a heard questionnaire unless approximate estimates are acceptable. An alternative is to translate interval level questions into ordinal questions.

Third, matrix questions are challenging for heard questions because the main question needs to be repeated for each question item. This can quickly become tedious for respondents, as shown in the example in Tables 3.11 and 3.12. Table 3.11 provides the read version, which can be answered by respondents very quickly. Table 3.12 provides the heard version, which takes considerably longer because the phrases 'Did your business collaborate', '*If yes*, were they located in', and each of the three locations 'your country, elsewhere in your country, outside your country' need to be repeated for every question item. If they are not repeated, errors can occur if respondents forget the purpose of the question or the response options. Therefore, for heard delivery methods, only a few matrix questions can be asked, the main question that is repeated needs to be short, and there should be no more than seven question items and preferably fewer.

Both face-to-face and CATI delivery methods for heard questionnaires have advantages that may outweigh these disadvantages. The CATI method can obtain responses quickly and may benefit from higher response rates than achievable through printed or online questionnaires (Lee et al., 2019). This is because an interview is more personal, and the interviewer may be more likely to reach the intended respondent. Online questionnaires can be rejected

Table 3.11   Read version of a matrix question (printed or online questionnaires viewed on a desktop, laptop, or tablet)

Did your business collaborate with each of the following types of organizations in the past year? If yes, where was your collaboration partner located?

(Tick all locations that apply)

	No	Yes	Your state	Elsewhere in [country]	Outside [country]
Other businesses within your business group	☐	☐	☐	☐	☐
Suppliers of equipment, materials, services or software	☐	☐	☐	☐	☐
Clients or customers	☐	☐	☐	☐	☐
Other businesses in your sector, including competitors	☐	☐	☐	☐	☐
Universities or other higher education institutions	☐	☐	☐	☐	☐

as spam or easily ignored, while administrative staff can prevent mailed questionnaires from being shown to a respondent. In some countries, face-to-face interviews are more acceptable for cultural reasons as they show greater personalization and respect. An interview can also overcome difficulties in accessing organizations in the informal sector and households that lack an online connection or reliable mail delivery. Finally, face-to-face interviews are better at eliciting answers to open questions, particularly for semi-structured questionnaires where almost all questions are open. If the answer to an open question is insufficient, the interviewer can probe for additional details.

3.7.2   Online (Web) Questionnaires

Online or web questionnaires are mixed method surveys because the questionnaire can be completed using a desktop/laptop, tablet or smartphone (Toepoel and Lugtig, 2022). The main difference across these devices is the size of the screen, with desktops and laptops capable of imitating the full page of a printed questionnaire, while smartphone screens are too small to replicate a printed questionnaire. Tablets lie in between. There are several commercial providers of software for producing and formatting online questionnaires and for collecting responses, including LimeSurvey, Survey Monkey, TypeForm and Qualtrics. Universities are likely to subscribe to one of them. A major advantage of online questionnaire software is that it automatically estimates the time required to answer the questions, drawing on data for millions of respondents to previous online questionnaires.

Table 3.12   Heard version of a matrix question (CATI or face-to-face)

READ OUT: The next question asks for a 'yes' or 'no' answer to whether your business collaborated with other types of organizations in the past year, and if yes, where your collaboration partner was located. Collaboration partners can be located in more than one region.	
Response categories for the interviewer: 1 = Yes, 2 = No, 7 = Don't know	
a) Did your business collaborate with other businesses within your business group?	1 2 7
If yes, were they located in:	
a1. Your state	1 2 7
a2. Elsewhere in your country	1 2 7
a3. Outside your country	1 2 7
b) Did your business collaborate with suppliers of equipment, materials, services or software?	1 2 7
If yes, were they located in:	
b1. Your state	1 2 7
b2. Elsewhere in your country	1 2 7
b3. Outside your country	1 2 7
c) Did your business collaborate with clients or customers	1 2 7
If yes, were they located in:	
c1. Your state	1 2 7
c2. Elsewhere in your country	1 2 7
c3. Outside your country	1 2 7
d) Did your business collaborate with other businesses in your sector, including competitors	1 2 7
If yes, were they located in:	
d1. Your state	1 2 7
d2. Elsewhere in your country	1 2 7
d3. Outside your country	1 2 7
e) Did your business collaborate with universities or other higher education institutions	1 2 7
If yes, were they located in:	
e1. Your state	1 2 7
e2. Elsewhere in your country	1 2 7
e3. Outside your country	1 2 7

If potential respondents choose the device for completing an online question-naire, which is often the case (section 5.2), you need to provide the question-naire in formats that are suitable for all types of devices: desktop/laptops, tablets and smartphones. Online survey software can do this automatically, but it is better to manually optimize smartphone and tablet versions to improve their appearance. This is essential for matrix questions that may not fully display the main question on a smartphone screen. The best option is to follow the CATI example given in Table 3.12, which repeats the main question and all response options in all question items. List questions need to be shorter if viewed on a smartphone screen (Brosnan et al., 2017), with preferably no more than seven items.

The use of smartphones creates other demands on questionnaire content and design. Due to the small screen size, the time to complete a questionnaire is between 15% to 40% longer on a smartphone than on other devices or a printed questionnaire (Liebe et al., 2015; Skeie et al., 2019; Toninelli and Revilla, 2020; Tourangeau et al., 2018). A common recommendation is that a smartphone survey should not take more than ten minutes, although this is based on data from commercial panels and university students (Sammut et al., 2021). Managers may be more forgiving and accept a longer questionnaire, but nevertheless brevity is likely to be more important for questionnaires that are delivered to a smartphone than for other delivery methods.

The best completion rates (no item non-responses) and data quality for matrix questions viewed on a computer or tablet are obtained when there are less than ten question items and preferably no more than five to seven (Grady et al., 2019). Reassuringly, the type of device used to complete an online survey has very little effect on data quality (Sandorf et al., 2022; Tourangeau et al., 2018).

Online surveys can take advantage of several features (see Box 3.1) that are usually unavailable in printed questionnaires for technical reasons or cost, such as high-quality photographs, interactive graphical enhancements or multiple colours. Other features include automated skip routines, a choice between page views and continuous scrolling to move through the questionnaire, dropdown menus and built-in definitions that are visible by hovering over a word or phrase.

As with printed questionnaires, the layout of response options in an online format should be consistent. It is common to use the round 'radio button' response format for online questions that permit only one correct answer out of a list or in a column, whereas check boxes are used when more than one item in a list can be selected.

BOX 3.1   FEATURES OF ONLINE QUESTIONNAIRES THAT ARE NOT POSSIBLE IN A PRINTED QUESTIONNAIRE

Page view: Only one page is visible. Pressing the return bar, tab or arrow moves to a new page. Often only one or two questions are provided per page.

Scrolling: The respondent moves through the questionnaire by using the arrows to scroll down or up the page, as in a text document. Scrolling is more common for smartphone devices than for desktops, laptops and tablets, which mostly use page views.

Automated skip routines (branch logic): Respondents are directed to different questions depending on their answer to previous questions. The software can also change a question based on previous responses, for example referring to the respondent's country or reported activities.

Dropdown (pop-up) menus: Question response options include a menu of items that can be selected. For instance, a dropdown menu for a question on gender could include 'male', 'female', 'other' and 'do not wish to answer'. Using dropdown menus for providing response options has little effect on the time required to answer a question, but it can result in an increase in errors when there is a long list of items, such as for country (Healey, 2007).

Built-in definitions: Definitions can be included in a hyperlink, in a dropdown menu that opens when the respondent rolls the cursor over a word (the respondent must actively request the definition), or directly next to the question in the main visual path. Placing the information directly after the question or in the question are the best options, as these increase the probability that the respondent reads and considers the definition when answering the question (Peytchev et al., 2010).

Graphical enhancements: These include short videos or interactive features such as drag-and-drop response methods (respondents drag an icon to a response column). They have very few benefits over text-only online formats (Dolnicar et al., 2013; Downes-Le Guin et al., 2012). Drag-and-drop formats for obtaining a response to a question increase respondent engagement, but the positive effects rapidly decrease, indicating that drag and drop should only be used sparingly (Sikkel et al., 2014).

Response reminders: Failure to answer a question can cause an automatic reminder that asks the respondent to return and complete the missed question. The reminder can be forced (the respondent cannot progress until the missed question is completed) or voluntary (the respondent can ignore the reminder and continue). Reminders reduce item non-response (Dillman and Smyth, 2007), but forced reminders should be used sparingly or not at all because they can cause respondents to abandon the questionnaire (Steiger et al., 2007).

Progress bars: A progress bar informs respondents how far they have progressed through the questionnaire. Progress bars are standard practice and come in three versions: constant progress (the indicator bar gives an accurate measure of the respondent's ongoing progress), a slow to fast indicator bar (the indicator starts out indicating slower than actual progress and speeds up over time), and a fast to slow indicator bar (the indicator shows rapid progress at first and gradually slows down). Experiments have found that the best method is to use a fast to slow progress bar, followed by a constant progress bar or no progress bar, but the differences are minor (Villar et al., 2013). The decision on the type of progress bar depends on the ethical views of the survey group.

Slider bars for ordinal questions: Slider bars permit the respondent to precisely select the importance or other characteristic of a Likert question, instead of being limited to discrete importance options such as 'very' or 'moderate' importance. Instead, the respondent moves a marker along a line between two points marking the ends, such as '0' for no importance and '7' for very high importance, with multiple gradations between an interval scale possible. The use of slider bars can more accurately reflect the respondent's opinion and reduce the problem of non-differentiated responses for scalar questions, most likely because it is considerably more difficult to give the same answer with a slider than with other response formats (Downes-Le Guin et al., 2012). The disadvantages are that slider bars are more time-consuming and therefore should only be used for a small number of questions and they are not practical for surveys answered on a smartphone.

In online surveys, interval level data for sales or employment can be pre-filled using other data sources, such as data obtained from a business register or from an annual report on a company website. The purpose of pre-filling is to reduce the burden for respondents, who only needs to check the accuracy of pre-filled data and revise as necessary. However, never pre-fill the responses to Likert and other questions that ask for perceptions.

Other good practices for online surveys are to use no more than four colours (lighter or darker shades of a colour count as separate colours) and to use them consistently, for instance one colour for the main question and another colour for question items in a list or matrix question. More colours are distracting. Screen resolution can be an issue with smartphones, requiring strong contrast between text and the background. Do not contradict common internet usage, for instance do not use blue or underline words unless they are a hyperlink.

It is very important to provide simple, easy-to-use procedures for saving responses and leaving a questionnaire on a device at any point and returning to it later. How to save and continue a questionnaire at a later time must be clearly explained in the email that includes the link to an online survey and at the start of the online questionnaire.

3.7.3 Comparability between Printed and Online Questionnaires

When the survey method uses online and printed questionnaires, the appearance and layout of the printed and online questionnaires must be as similar as possible to minimize differences in how respondents interpret questions. This severely constrains the use of many of the unique features of online surveys, as described in Box 3.1. Instead, the online version must not use dropdown menus for response options, hyperlinks or dropdown menus for definitions, graphical enhancements, slider bars, or page views that provide a single question item for matrix questions. Response bars and reminders can be used in the online version as these two methods do not influence interpretation of the questions or how they are answered, unlike the use of slider bars, which does affect the answer.

The two most serious issues for comparability between printed and online formats are the presentation of matrix questions and the use of automated skip routines.

A printed questionnaire cannot use a separate page per question item in a matrix question, for instance on the frequency of different activities, as in an online questionnaire. To maintain comparability, the online version should use the full matrix question as presented in the printed version (Dillman and Smyth, 2007), but this is not possible on a smartphone if the matrix question does not fit into the screen. You may need to accept a small difference between responses by smartphone versus other methods, or try to encourage respondents not to answer the questionnaire by smartphone (section 5.2).

Automated skip routines are an advantage of online surveys because they reduce respondent burden. Respondents do not see skipped questions and do not need to follow instructions to find the next question to answer. Skip routines in a printed version increase respondent burden because the respondents see – and may consider – questions that they are directed to skip and they must carefully follow the skip instructions.

The fact that respondents to a printed questionnaire can see questions that a filter question directs them to skip, whereas online respondents do not, can lead to possible differences in responses. For instance, respondents to a printed questionnaire could obtain information from skipped questions that causes them to return to questions before the filter and change one or more answers. An option to improve comparability is to 'grey' skipped questions in an online survey so that they are still visible to the respondent although not answerable. This option depends on the capabilities of the online survey software. Respondents to tests of internet surveys have been observed revising questions before the filter after seeing greyed questions (Potaka, 2008). However, there is no research on how often this occurs and if the use of greyed versus hidden skipped questions makes a notable difference to the collected data.

3.8   MINIMIZING UNDESIRABLE RESPONDENT BEHAVIOUR

Multiple characteristics of the questionnaire, including question design and content, question format, and the questionnaire layout can reduce undesirable respondent behaviours that increase item non-response or reduce data quality.

'Satisficing' refers to respondent behaviours to reduce the time and effort required to complete a questionnaire. These include abandoning the survey before it is completed (premature termination or dropout), skipping questions, 'non-differentiation' from giving the identical response option in a matrix question, for example answering 'slightly important' to all questions or 'straightlining' (Couper et al., 2013), and speeding through the questionnaire (Barge and Gehlbach, 2012; Downes-Le Guin et al., 2012). Another satisficing strategy is to select the neutral or mid category, which is more common among respondents with low motivation (Lenzner, 2012).

Premature termination and skipping questions reduce the amount of data that are collected without necessarily affecting the quality of elicited responses, while non-differentiation and speeding can reduce quality and lower the criterion validity, or the ability of questions to predict dependent variables (Peytchev and Peytcheva, 2017). Invalid or meaningless data can be caused by inattentive, careless or random responses due to satisficing behaviour (Barge and Gehlbach, 2012; Leiner, 2019). Meaningless responses are a more serious issue than missing data because they can produce Type 1 errors where a true null hypothesis is rejected and Type 2 errors where an incorrect null hypothesis is not rejected. However, a few meaningless responses due to satisficing behaviours are less important for producing Type 1 and 2 errors than poor question wording, which can produce considerably more meaningless responses, and problems with sampling, such as non-random sampling and low response rates (Leiner, 2019).

The three main features of questionnaire design that can minimize undesirable behaviours are (1) reduce the length of the questionnaire, (2) ensure that the questionnaire and individual questions are of interest to the respondents, and (3) use appropriate question formats, such as altering response formats to keep the respondent's attention and limiting the number of question items in list and matrix questions.

Long questionnaires are more susceptible to undesirable respondent behaviour than short questionnaires (Barge and Gehlbach, 2012; Herzog and Bachman, 1981). Questions that occur later in a long questionnaire are more likely to experience a decline in quality due to respondent boredom or waning motivation that results in skim-reading questions instead of careful reading (Galesic and Bosnjak, 2009). Matrix questions are more susceptible to non-differentiation such as straightlining than other question formats. The same issue of waning respondent interest applies to long lists of 'yes/no' or check list questions. There is no difference in non-differentiation behaviour between printed and online questionnaires for items arranged in a matrix (Kim et al., 2019).

When an online survey is not combined with printed questionnaires, slider bars for ordinal questions can reduce non-differentiated responses, particularly for questions located at the end of a questionnaire (Downes-Le Guin et al., 2012), but they are difficult to use if respondents are replying on a smartphone or tablet without a mouse. Online versions of a matrix question can reduce satisficing behaviour and interitem correlation by using a separate page view for each question, so that the respondent must assess each question separately, without immediate reference to other questions in a matrix. An alternative solution to the satisficing issue for both printed and online questionnaires is to include no more than seven to nine question items in the matrix question. This may require a long matrix question to be broken up into several questions on different topics. For instance, a long question on obstacles could be divided into one matrix question on internal obstacles within the unit and a second matrix question on external obstacles.

Meaningless responses can be reduced through analysis of the data after the survey is completed to detect satisficing behaviour (section 2.3) or by including marker questions in the questionnaire, such as non-sensical questions ('have you ever used a computer?) or questions for which the ordinal response categories are switched, so that a 'high' response category that is normally used to identify 'intensive use of an activity' is switched to identify low use of an activity (Burns and Christiansen, 2011). The goal of these questions is to prod respondents to stay alert, but they could also annoy respondents, resulting in skipped questions. Due to possible issues with the use of marker questions, a better option is to conduct post-survey analyses to identify satisficing behaviour.

3.9   CONCLUSIONS

The question design, content and layout of a questionnaire will affect respondent comprehension, questionnaire and item response rates, and data quality. Response rates and data quality can be increased by following good question design and layout principles and by ensuring that the question content is interesting and relevant to respondents. Involving key stakeholders in the early design and review of the questionnaire can help to reduce response burden and increase relevance (Fulton, 2018).

A summary of good practice for all questionnaire formats (CATI, face-to-face, online and printed) is as follows:

1. Carefully think through research questions to ensure that all necessary data are collected while excluding questions that are not relevant or simply 'nice to know'.
2. If multivariate analysis will be conducted, collect multiple versions of the dependent variable in case one or more fail.
3. Provide a time period covered by the questions, such as 'currently', 'in the last month' or 'in the last year'.
4. Keep the questionnaire short and easy to understand so that it can be answered in 15 minutes or less, or ten minutes or less for questionnaires that will be completed on a smartphone. Minimize the number of demanding numeric (interval and percentage) and open questions.
5. Evaluate all questions and question items to make sure that they do not include more than one question and ensure that questions in a list or matrix do not overlap or cover similar concepts or activities.
6. Vary the measurement level and response categories to increase respondent interest and to avoid common method bias.
7. Do not use more than seven to nine sub-questions in a matrix question. Split up matrix questions into separate themes if necessary.
8. After a small number of questions on the respondent such as their work experience, begin with questions that are interesting to respondents. Where possible, place less interesting questions at the end.

Five additional good practices apply to read questionnaires (printed and online):

1. Do not rely on respondents to read separate definitions. Wherever possible, include definitions in the question.
2. Do not crowd questions – include generous white or 'blank' space.
3. Use a consistent choice of response formats by question type, such as radio buttons for lists where only one option can be selected and check boxes when multiple options can be selected.
4. Ensure good contrast between the text and background and use fonts of 11 point or greater. Do not use distracting layout features.
5. Keep the line width for the main questions at no more than two-thirds across the page (this does not apply to smartphones), but response options can cross the entire page.

Four additional good practices only apply to online questionnaires:

1. A text-only format is probably the best format for organizational surveys, with few advantages to using graphical enhancements.
2. Skip routines should be invisible to the respondent.
3. Do not use forced responses, although an error message or warning for an incomplete question is good practice.
4. Do not use more than four colours and do not use blue or underlining for words unless they are for a hyperlink.

One additional good practice applies to combined printed/online questionnaires:

1. As much as possible, maintain comparability in question format and design, for instance by 'greying' skipped questions in the online version and using similar matrix question formats. The latter may not be possible on a smartphone.

There are many useful online resources for readers who want additional information. As an example, the Australian Bureau of Statistics provides a useful website that covers good practices for question design and layout.[1]

NOTE

1. www.abs.gov.au/websitedbs/d3310114.nsf/home/Basic+Survey+Design+-+ Questionnaire+Design

4. Questionnaire testing

4.1 INTRODUCTION

Pre-testing a questionnaire is essential for minimizing errors from respondents misunderstanding a question or being unable to provide an accurate response (Willis, 2018). It is very common for questions that appear simple and obvious to the person who wrote the question to be anything but for respondents. To illustrate the problem, Table 4.1 provides two examples of problematic questions taken from real surveys. Both questions underwent cognitive testing, but in each case either the number of interviews or the level of probing did not identify the problem. Take a moment to see if you can identify what is wrong with each of these questions.

The problem with the first question was not identified until the survey was almost completed, when a respondent phoned the survey manager to ask if 'worldwide' included domestic sales or only referred to non-domestic sales. In a panic, the survey manager checked other responses and discovered, based on corporate data available from other sources, that some respondents had interpreted 'worldwide' to mean international only while other respondents had interpreted it to include domestic sales. It was impossible to determine how the question was interpreted when the reported sales for 'worldwide' was larger than the reported sales for domestic. Correcting the error was expensive, with hundreds of businesses telephoned to obtain the correct data.

The second question is trickier. The error wasn't found until data analysis noted inexplicably large differences in the responses to this question by managers who reported collaboration with other firms in a previous question versus those who did not report collaboration. The problem was due to the lack of a comma in the question. The intention was for respondents to understand the question as:

> Does your business share the new technologies that it has developed, with other firms or institutions?

In other words, the business developed the new technologies on its own and then shared them. In the original version without the comma, business managers who reported collaboration interpreted the question as referring to technologies that

Table 4.1   Examples of problematic questions

1. What was your firm's domestic and worldwide sales in 2020?		
		Don't Know
Domestic	_____,000	☐
Worldwide	_____,000	☐
2. Does your business share the new technologies that it has developed with other firms or institutions?		
	Yes	☐
	No	☐

were collaboratively developed with other firms or organizations, while managers who did not report collaboration interpreted the question as developing new technologies that were developed without the help of other organizations.

The problems with most questions are not as subtle as these two examples, but nevertheless many minor and major errors in questions can be missed by the individuals or teams that developed them. Pre-testing a questionnaire before its use in a survey is an essential step to produce a high-quality questionnaire that obtains good-quality data.

There are three types of pre-testing: getting your colleagues, experts or friends to read and comment on drafts of your questionnaire, cognitive testing involving face-to-face interviews with a small number of ten to 50 individuals drawn from the population of interest, and a pilot survey of between 50 and 300 individuals randomly drawn from the population of interest. The first type of testing is easy to do and is essential. Conversely, both cognitive testing and a pilot survey are time-consuming and incur costs, which unfortunately can lead researchers to skip one or both methods (Converse and Presser, 1986). If you are short of funds or time, skip the pilot survey, but never skip the cognitive testing, which is essential to achieve two important goals for questionnaire design: all respondents interpret each question as intended, and all respondents can provide reasonably accurate responses to each question. Meeting these goals is necessary to obtain reliable and valid results (section 2.4.1).

4.1.1   Testing by Colleagues, Friends, etc.

As a first step, ask colleagues or friends to provide written or oral comments on draft versions of your questionnaire. The goal is to identify as many problems as possible before moving to the more expensive and time-consuming testing methods (Forsyth and Lessler, 1991). Common problems that can be identified at this stage include spelling errors, questions or questionnaires that are too long, too complicated, or too demanding, logical inconsistencies, the use of questions hidden within other questions (double questions), and inaccurate or incomplete skip routines. However, colleagues may not be sensitive to overly demanding, complicated questions or the use of specialized vocabulary.

Early drafts of your questionnaire can be tested by colleagues and friends without consideration of the question layout, but later drafts for testing by colleagues and friends should use the format that you intend to use in your survey (telephone, interview, printed or online). If you have skip routines, ask your colleagues and friends to take on different personas to test your routines in a near final draft for this stage of testing. Every possible combination of skip routines should be tested several times, and more frequently for questionnaires that will be implemented using CATI or online survey methods where the missed questions are not heard or not visible.

4.2   COGNITIVE TESTING

Cognitive testing can identify complicated and demanding questions and the use of specialized vocabulary, but its main purpose is to determine if specific questions will obtain accurate, meaningful and comparable data from potential respondents and if not, how to improve them (Collins, 2003; Willis, 1999). This section provides an overview of cognitive testing, but Willis (2005) is a useful resource for those who would like additional details and practical instruction.

Cognitive testing is the gold standard for question design, but it is not perfect. It can miss issues with a questionnaire, particularly if only a few interviews are conducted, as in the examples at the start of this chapter. Furthermore, volunteers for cognitive testing often have an above average interest and enthusiasm in the topics covered by the questions compared to the population of interest. This gives them greater motivation to understand a question, resulting in a failure to identify problems that will impede less motivated respondents.

The theory behind cognitive testing assumes that respondents use four cognitive processes to answer survey questions: trying to understand what a question is asking, finding the relevant information in their memory, making a judgement about the information, and adapting the information to fit into the response format provided by the question (Tourangeau, 1984). Cognitive testing identifies problems associated with these cognitive processes (Jobe and Herrmann, 1996). The goal is to gain insight into which questions pose problems, which terms are misunderstood, and where questions might be inappropriate, insufficient or written in a way that leads to misunderstandings or satisficing behaviour (Qureschi and Rowlands, 2004). This form of testing provides a way to address difficulties in designing questionnaires and to minimize response error due to question wording, the format of the questionnaire and the order of questions.

The use of cognitive testing to improve questionnaires helps meet several quality criteria for questions discussed in section 2.5.1: face validity (the questionnaire addresses the right issues from the perspective of the respondent), content validity (the responses measure what the researchers want to measure), inter-rater reliability (similar responses across respondents), reliability (high sensitivity or few false negatives and high specificity or few false positives in how respondents answer the questions), temporal accuracy (measures changes over time, when relevant), and minimal desirability (low social desirability or other forms of bias).

Cognitive testing is a powerful tool that can lead to minor or major revisions or to the rejection of a question (DeMaio et al., 1993; Lessler et al., 1989; Willis et al., 1999). As an example, 18 questions in the draft Co-Val questionnaire on user involvement in public sector innovations underwent six rounds of testing with colleagues who were experts on the topic before proceeding to two phases of cognitive testing. Five questions failed cognitive testing and were not included in the final questionnaire, three required major revisions, nine required minor revisions, and only one question did not need any revisions at all (Arundel et al., 2019).

A serious challenge for data quality is when survey respondents answer a question that they do not understand or know the answer to (Collins, 2003), reducing reliability through false positive or negative responses. A hypothetical example would be a question to business managers on whether or not their business is using blockchain technology. 'Blockchain' is widely discussed in the media, but it is very likely that a share of business managers do not understand what blockchain is. A percentage of managers could incorrectly answer the question with a 'yes' (a false positive), on the assumption that this is an important technology and therefore their company must be using it. To avoid this problem, the term 'blockchain' would need to be defined through widely understandable language. Cognitive testing is then required to make sure that the description of a blockchain is correctly understood by almost all respondents and that they can give an accurate response, even if the response is 'no'.

Moreover, cognitive interviewing allows researchers to identify inconsistencies, unclear terms or questions, inappropriate response options, formatting problems as well as to record respondents' reactions (Noel and Prizeman, 2005). Cognitive testing interviewees can also be asked if they find anything of importance missing in a matrix or list question.

4.2.1 Cognitive Interview Methods

Two techniques can be used in a cognitive interview, either separately or together: 'think-aloud' and question probes.

In the think-aloud interview, respondents are asked to describe how they reached their answer (what they were thinking) as they answer each question. This method is demanding of interviewees, who must also be comfortable with continuously describing their thoughts. Alternatively, the interviewer asks probing questions after the interviewee completes a question. These questions are used to clarify the process used by respondents to answer a question and their understanding of specific terms, instructions and questions; respondent confidence in the accuracy of their answer, the knowledge that the respondent uses to answer, and if the response options were appropriate or easy to understand (Noel and Prizeman, 2005). The interviewer can also ask probes in response to the actions of a respondent, by asking, for example: 'I noticed you hesitated before answering that question, what were you thinking about?' Section 4.4.2 below gives examples of common probes.

4.2.2   Preparation for Cognitive Testing

Before the interviews begin, the researcher needs to select individuals to be interviewed, identify and train interviewers, and prepare an interview protocol. These tasks can be conducted concurrently.

Selecting interviewees

Interviewees do not need to be randomly selected. The most important criterion for selection is to ensure that interviewees cover a diversity of relevant characteristics of the target population that could influence the research questions (Converse and Presser, 1986). For instance, if the research question concerns human resource practices to support diversity in large businesses, the interviewees should include human resource managers from businesses in different sectors (services, manufacturing, construction, etc.) and with different ownership structures (privately held, listed on the stock market, part of a holding company). Depending on the topic, it may also be relevant to obtain interviewees that differ by gender, age or migrant background.

The number of cognitive interviews is usually between five and 15 per phase of testing (Willis, 2005), but there are exceptions, with studies with over 50 or 100 interviews (Arundel et al., 2019; Davis et al., 2001). The number of interviewees required increases with the number of organizational or personal characteristics that need to be covered to obtain a sufficient diversity of interviewees. You should have a minimum of one interviewee per characteristic of interest and preferably two. Consequently, if you have ten characteristics of interest you should plan for 20 interviewees. As most cognitive interviews require two phases, estimate the need for a second phase at half the number of interviews as the first phase.

The number of required interviewees increases substantially for surveys that will be conducted in two or more countries that speak different languages, as the questions will need to be tested in each national language. Under some conditions it may be possible to use a widely known second language, for instance if a very high percentage of the target population has excellent reading (for internet or printed questionnaires) or aural skills (for telephone or face-to-face interviews) in the second language and if the research question covers a topic where the second language is widely used. Examples where these criteria are probably met include a survey in English on the marketing activities of large businesses in the Netherlands and Scandinavia or a survey in French of managers at government ministries in Francophone Africa.

Research shows that there is a strong positive relationship between the number of identified problems with a questionnaire and the number of interviews (Blair et al., 1994). Some problems with a questionnaire will be rapidly identified by multiple interviewees, while others will only be picked up by a small number or possibly only one interviewee. A small number of interviews can miss many different types of problems, including serious ones. Plan for a minimum of ten cognitive interviews and preferably more.

In practice, the cognitive testing goal that all respondents can understand and give accurate responses to all questions is unlikely to be met, in part because there are always respondents who will misunderstand one or more questions, no matter how well designed, but cognitive testing should ensure that the goals for comprehension and accuracy are met for a large majority of your survey respondents.

Selection and training of interviewers
Good interviewers need to meet three requirements: knowledge of the research question and the purpose of all questions in the questionnaire, good inter-personal skills, such as the ability to put a subject at ease and always remain calm and pleasant during an interview, and some familiarity with bias and other factors that could detrimentally affect the interview. It is vitally important that the interviewer never expresses judgement, comments on nor criticizes the responses or concerns of the interviewee.

Interviewers need to be trained to acquire the necessary skills for cognitive testing. Familiarity with the purpose of the questions can be acquired through their inclusion in early questionnaire design meetings and, if possible, participation in meetings where interviewers discuss the results of cognitive testing and attendance at cognitive interviews as an observer. The interviewers must thoroughly understand the purpose of each question, otherwise they will not be able to judge if a response is adequate and when additional probing is necessary.

Potential interviewers with no previous experience of cognitive testing should take part in several role-playing trial interviews of the questionnaire to learn how to present themselves at the start of an interview, how to ask probing questions that can detect problems, and ensure that they maintain neutrality throughout an interview. The interviewer should also develop a few questions for the interviewee to include in the role play. Different colleagues can take on the role of an interviewee. The role of each interviewee should be supported by a description, not divulged to the interviewer, of the colleague's imaginary position and information on their business or other type of organization. A role-playing example for cognitive testing is given in Annex 4.1.

The person with the best knowledge of the research questions and the purpose of all questions is likely to be the person leading the project or who has had the largest role in designing the questionnaire. However, this person would be entirely unsuited to take part in the interviews if they react defensively to interviewee criticisms of their questions or a failure to understand a question as intended. The purpose of the interview is to identify flaws in the questions or format and for this to happen the interviewees must feel comfortable in raising concerns or problems.

Cognitive interviewing requires an unhurried pace that is largely controlled by the interviewee, who may spend considerable time explaining how they interpret a question or digress off-topic. Cognitive interviewers must be comfortable with departing from the planned interview structure when this occurs. Efforts to steer the interviewee need to be gently handled, as the interviewee needs to feel in control over the pace. If the questionnaire format and skip routines are preliminary, the interviewee should be asked at the start of the interview to concentrate on the meaning of specific questions and ignore formatting issues.

4.3   PROTOCOL FOR OBTAINING INTERVIEWEES AND INTERVIEW QUESTIONS

The protocol consists of the interview design and the questions to be covered.

4.3.1   Interview Design

The protocol for the interview design should include information on contacting potential interviewees, the approximate timing of the interviews, and the necessary documents.

Inclusion criteria
The criteria for ensuring a diversity of potential interviewees, such as the type of business or organization, management level, etc.

Contact log
This is usually maintained in a spreadsheet program and is necessary to maintain a clear and complete record of all contact attempts, including the date you attempt to make contact and comments on the results of the attempt (examples include no response, out of the office, call back (date), interview date and location, etc.). Assign an identification number to each potential interviewee in the contact log.

List of contacts
A preliminary list of the names and details of individuals to be contacted is needed. Personal contacts such as acquaintances (do not use friends), parents of children's classmates, and neighbours can be used as interviewees if they meet the inclusion criteria. The contact list should be four or five times longer than the number of interviews that you plan to conduct, as many contacts are likely to refuse to participate. In addition, 10% to 20% may have to withdraw after an interview time has been set up, due to work pressures or other reasons. You should account for the latter by arranging more interviews than you need, although you must conduct all interviews if no one drops out.

Contact method
The protocol needs to describe the method (post or email) for sending interviewees an invitation letter to participate and follow-up rules for interviewees who do not reply to the first contact. Invitation letters sent by post are more likely to be successful than invitation letters sent by email.

Invitation letter
The main objective of the invitation letter is to convince the recipient that their participation in a cognitive interview will be an interesting experience and vital to the success of the survey. The letter needs to briefly outline the purpose of the interview, a motivation for why their participation is important and appreciation for their participation, an offer of confidentiality, the length of time of the interview (no more than one hour), and that the recipient can choose the location, although this is usually their workplace. The invitation letter should also state approximately when you will be calling to request participation and set up a meeting. The letter may instruct the recipient on how they can contact you to either accept or decline to participate or to obtain more information, but this makes it easier for the recipient to decline than if you call them by phone. Annex 4.2 gives an example of a contact letter for cognitive testing.

Follow-up phone call
Contact potential interviewees by phone no more than two days after they were likely to receive the invitation letter. A phone call is much more effective in

convincing people to participate than further correspondence by email or post. If you use up the number of advance contacts before obtaining sufficient interviewees, send out a second round of invitation letters. You may need a third and fourth round. For this reason, it is important to keep a good contact log.

The protocol should include the contents to be discussed in a personal phone call with potential interviewees. Gaining the person's cooperation depends on the ability of the researcher to establish rapport with the person during the first few seconds of the call. To help ensure a successful outcome, one must prepare for the call. In this initial personal contact, the first task is to explain who you are and why you are calling. You can then give additional information about the interview, their expected involvement and confidentiality. Emphasize that the interviewee does not need to prepare anything before the interview – the only demand on their time is the interview itself.

Potential interviewees will often ask to see a copy of the questionnaire in advance. You may provide a short description (a few sentences) of the topics to be covered, but never agree to send a copy of the questionnaire before the interview. Cognitive testing requires that you probe for issues the first time the interviewee sees the questionnaire, as this is the most similar environment experienced by respondents to the full survey – who are unlikely to review the questionnaire first before completing it. You may provide this explanation to potential interviewees as the reason why you are not providing the questions in advance.

When a person agrees to be interviewed, fix a date and location that is convenient for the interviewee and obtain their email address if you contacted them by phone. You may propose approximate time slots and days that fit into your existing interview plan, but be prepared to accept other time slots that the interviewee suggests.

Your contact may give one or more reasons for declining an interview. You may use the call to try to convert a refusal into an acceptance, for instance by stressing the value of their participation. Table 4.2 lists common reasons for refusing and the approach you can take to change people's minds.

Phases and timing
The protocol should include the number of planned phases (usually two), the approximate number of interviews in each phase, and the planned dates and time span for each phase. The required time span depends on the number of interviews you plan to conduct, the time for each interview and the time to travel from one interview to another. A good practice is to allot two hours after an interview so that the interviewers can type up their notes while the interview is fresh in their minds. This will limit the number of interviews to approximately two per day, but it may be possible to squeeze in three interviews if

Table 4.2   Converting refusals obtained by phone or letter

Reasons for refusing	Ways to gain cooperation
Too busy/calling at an inconvenient time	Give the respondent a choice of times that you can call back, for example, 'I'm sorry I called you at an inconvenient time. Would it be better if I called you back (in the evening, morning, etc.)?'
Misunderstanding the purpose of the study	Provide a short overview and how their participation can help.
Legitimacy of the study	Give the name of the funding organization for the study, where the study is being conducted (university, government agency, etc.), support you may have from professional groups, etc.
Why me?	Explain the selection process and refer by name to anyone who might have suggested them. Also emphasize the need for a diverse range of participants, etc., for instance state that 'your contribution would be greatly appreciated as we are missing someone with your expertise and background'.
Time or cost to participate	This is largely time. Emphasize the value of their participation, such as the number of people who will receive the final questionnaire and the importance of getting it right.
Fears about use of the data	Explain the confidentiality agreement and that you are not collecting data on their answers to the questions but are only interested in how they understand the questions or problems that they might identify in the questions.

travel distances are short. An alternative is to conduct four interviews in one day and keep the following day free to type up the notes.

Confidentiality
Confidentiality must be offered in both the invitation letter and by the interviewers at the start of the interview. One must assure interviewees that their names and any information collected from them will be held in the strictest confidence, will only be used for the purposes of the study and will never be released in any form that would allow the interviewee or their employer to be identified.

Protecting confidentiality means that information about individual interviewees is not made available to anyone outside the immediate research project team. Access to identifying information must be limited to as few people as possible. Summary information of the results to be shared with the research team should have identifier information removed and only provide basic information such as the type of organization or its size (large or small).

Follow-on emails
Once accepted, send a confirmation email for the date, time, location and purpose of the interview within a day of the personal phone call. Send another email reminder a few days before the arranged meeting date (Annex 4.3 provides an example of a reminder).

Informed consent form
This may be required as part of an ethics requirement. The interviewee should be asked to sign the form after the purpose of the cognitive testing has been explained, but before the interview begins. The contents of this form may vary by local requirements. An example of an informed consent form for cognitive testing is provided in Annex 4.4. The form should be adapted to the requirements of your ethics committee. The example in Annex 4.4 is very thorough, but other ethics committees could be satisfied with a shorter form.

4.3.2   Questions to be Covered

The interview should not exceed one hour as the process is demanding for both the interviewer and the interviewees. Moreover, subjects vary in their overall speed and the detail they provide on questions and to probing. The interview process should be flexible and not require interviewees to cover all questions if time runs out.

Only a limited number of questions can be covered in a one-hour interview because interviewees need time to comment on each question. The number of questions that can be covered depends on the difficulty of the questions, with more time required for questions asking for interval level data and matrix questions with multiple sub-questions. When there is a mix of question types, the maximum number of questions is approximately 20 and they should fit, with a lot of blank space, on no more than nine or ten pages. The limit for more difficult questions or matrix questions is approximately 12 questions on five or six pages.

If there are more than 20 mixed types of questions in a questionnaire, some questions will need to be dropped from cognitive testing or the questions divided into two groups, with each group of questions tested on separate interviewees. The questions may also need to be divided into two or more groups if the interviews frequently run out of time before all questions are tested.

Do not make the mistake of assuming that questions that seem easy for you or your colleagues will not need to undergo cognitive testing. Only very simple questions that have been used and cognitively tested in other research can be dropped, such as questions on the gender or highest educational level obtained by the respondent. Many questions that have been used in other research may not have undergone previous testing (Converse and Presser, 1986) or they could have drawn interviewees from a different population, for instance businesses instead of a planned study population of public sector managers. These questions will also need to be cognitively tested.

4.4   CONDUCTING COGNITIVE INTERVIEWS

4.4.1   Preparation

It is possible for one person to conduct the interview, but it is best if there are two interviewers. In many countries it is best to have interviewers of different gender. With two interviewers, one should ask the probing questions and take notes when possible while the other should only take notes. This can alternate during the interview, for instance interviewer A asks the probing questions for the first question and interviewer B primarily takes notes, while for the second question interviewer B asks the questions and interviewer A primarily takes notes (Converse and Presser, 1986).

Several materials are required for the interviews:

1.   An interview control log with names of interviewees, their title (manager, director, etc.) and contact information (the telephone numbers you will use to contact the interviewees).
2.   If designed to be read (online or on paper), sufficient printed copies of the questions for all interviewees.
3.   If designed to be heard, a written version of the questions designed for a CATI or face-to-face interview. These can be kept on paper or on a tablet or laptop.
4.   Additional blank sheets.
5.   Pens.

Examples of the questionnaire form for the interviewee and interviewer for a printed or online version are given in Annex 4.5. The interviewee version only includes the questions to be tested, while the version for the interviewer includes sufficient space for handwritten notes and prompts. A good method is to print the interviewer form as a booklet, with the questions and prompts on the left-hand side and space to make notes on the right-hand side.

The use of a laptop or tablet to make notes is not recommended because it is less personal, is more difficult for the interviewer to make eye contact with the interviewee, and the noise of typing can be distracting, even on laptops with minimal typing noise.

The interview control log should be kept updated and include information on when the interview took place (date) and the duration of the interview.

4.4.2   The Interview

The interviewer should arrive for the interview at exactly the agreed time. On the rare occasion when you expect to be more than a few minutes late, phone ahead and provide the interviewee with a revised starting time.

The first few minutes of the interview are fundamental to its success (Salant and Dillman, 1994). Use a friendly but neutral tone that builds rapport with the interviewee and a moderate pace. Know what you will say before the interview but avoid memorizing your lines. It must sound easy and relaxed. The interviewers need to first introduce themselves, briefly state the purpose of the interview, reiterate the confidentiality agreement and ask for an informed consent document to be signed (if required). Then ask the interviewee about their organization and their role, which will help to put them at ease. Almost everyone likes to talk about what they do, and it may help during the interview to refer to their role in the organization.

Request permission if you want to record the interview, but written notes must be made as recording equipment can be relied upon to fail. (All recording equipment follows Murphy's law – if something can go wrong, it will.) Furthermore, it is much faster to type up written notes than to listen to a full recording. The main value of a recording is to check handwritten notes, for instance if there is a disagreement between two interviewers, to clarify a result that was not fully captured in the notes, and to have a back-up in case notes are damaged.

The interviewers should also cover the following points in their introduction:

- Inform the interviewee that they are not collecting data and will use none of the answers to the questions. The purpose is to test the questions to identify those that may be difficult to understand, hard to answer, or that make little sense.
- State that the main objective is to explore how the interviewee arrives at an answer and the problems they encounter. Therefore, any detailed help the interviewee can give to the interviewer is of interest, even if it seems irrelevant or trivial.
- If necessary, the interviewer can state that they didn't write the questions, so the interviewee should freely criticize them. This helps to 'bring out' subjects who may otherwise be sensitive about being critical.

Next, explain the interview process and tell the interviewee that they are free to ask questions if they don't understand a term or are confused by the question or think that it should be asked differently. The introduction should be concise and short.

The format of the questions given to the interviewee must match the format for the planned full survey. For example, if the full survey will be conducted as a CATI survey, read each question aloud. Never allow the interviewee to see the written version of the question if the survey is designed for a telephone interview since the actual respondents will not have the opportunity to read the question. If the survey will be mailed or provided online, provide a similar version of the question layout that they would receive either on a printed questionnaire or on a web page.

The purpose of the interviews is not to get responses to questions, but to determine if the interviewees can understand and answer the questions. However, the interviewees should be asked to complete each question. Seeing which response options are used can guide probing, and the response data are useful for determining the boundaries of categorical response options using percentages etc.

There are two general options for working through the questions:

1. The interviewee is given time to read and answer all questions on the form. The time required to answer each question is recorded on the questionnaire response form for interviewers. Once finished, the interviewer returns to the first question and asks the interviewee to explain how they understood each question and its response options.
2. Alternatively, each question is answered and discussed in turn. The interviewee can use the think-aloud method as they answer the question, if they are comfortable with this, or after completing each question describe their understanding of the question and its response options (Davis and DeMaio, 1993).

Work through the questions slowly, first giving the interviewee time to describe how they understood the question in their own words. Often, the interviewee's responses will cover some of the probing questions. Once the interviewee has finished a question, ask probing questions that the interviewee did not address. Interviewees can also be asked for suggestions on missing questions that would be of value to include in the questionnaire.

The interviewee should do 90% or more of the talking. The interviewer rarely needs to speak other than for simple directions – 'please move to the next question', to signal a transition – 'the next few questions ask you about [topic X]', or to ask probing questions. The interviewer should never explain the questions, discuss the interviewee's responses (other than to ask additional probing questions), or introduce any additional information that may change the meaning of a question or bias a response.

When the interviewee has already provided information that probably answers the next question, the interviewer may preface the question with some combination of the following phrases:

> 'I know we've talked about this' or 'I know you just mentioned this, but I need to ask each question as it appears in the questionnaire.'
> 'You have already touched on this, but let me ask you ... .'
> 'You've told me something about this, but this next question asks ... .'

Potentially difficult questions are those that cover a long time span or an event that occurs in the past (over three months before the interview) or asks for financial information such as expenditures on an activity. For these questions, the interviewer needs to pay close attention to the consistency and accuracy of the response and the amount of effort that is required by the interviewee to answer the question. The interviewer should also ask the interviewee to estimate the accuracy of their answer. For instance, an interviewee can be asked to give an error margin around their estimate of an expenditure, such as plus or minus 10%.

Interviewers should make notes directly on their version of the interview questions for each interviewee. If necessary, ask the interviewee to slow down if they are talking too quickly. Wherever possible, the notes should include direct quotes of the interviewee. If there is insufficient space on your page for the interviewee's answer, use the margins (top, side or bottom), but be sure to clearly label the continuation of your notes.

Probing

For some questions, you may need to probe to make sure the interviewee understands the terms and the meaning of the question or response categories. You may also need to probe to determine how accurately interviewees think they can answer a question, particularly for difficult questions.

Before you begin cognitive testing, you may already be concerned about potential issues, such as terms or descriptions of an activity that might be misunderstood, or requests for information that interviewees might find difficult to give. Specific prompts for these questions should be included on the question form for the interviewers. Examples of prompts are included in Annex 4.5.

Use neutral probes that do not suggest a particular answer to the interviewee. Probes should also be used whenever the interviewee is hesitant to answer a question, seems to have trouble expressing themselves, appears too shy to speak, or whenever the interviewer thinks that the interviewee has not given a complete report of their thinking.

Table 4.3   *Common cognitive probes*

Cognitive probe	Example
Comprehension/interpretation probe	What does the term 'XXX' mean to you?
Paraphrasing	Can you repeat the question in your own words?
Confidence in answer	How confident are you in your answer ...?
Recall probe	How do you remember that ...?
Specific probe	Why do you think that ...?
General probes	How did you arrive at that answer?
	Was that easy or hard to answer?
	I noticed that you hesitated. Tell me what you were thinking.

Source: Willis (2005).

If you receive a 'depends' or 'qualified' answer, such as 'it depends on how many staff we have available', probe to find more information about the factors that influence their answer. Common probes are listed in Table 4.3.

Where possible, the interviews should be conducted in person, but if necessary, interviews can be conducted through a video call. The use of prompt questions about potential problems with the questions is very important in video interviews because interviewers may be unable to pick up body language or facial expressions that indicate problems with a question. Otherwise, proceed in the same manner as for a face-to-face interview.

4.4.3   Completing the Interview and Immediately Afterwards

Once you have completed all questions for which you have time, ask the interviewee if there is anything else they would like to ask or tell you. Before leaving, thank the interviewee for taking time to answer the questions and for participating in the project. Leave a business card with your name and business contact details in case the interviewee wishes to contact you afterwards.

Post-interview activities include recording the duration of the interview in the interview control log and typing and revising the notes as needed in an electronic format. Include comments or reactions, such as what went well, what did not go well, distractions, etc., reviewing all notes and filling in any gaps in the interviewee's responses, and ensuring that all identified problems encountered in the questions are clearly described and summarized.

Keep the original question pages with your notes in a safe place and ensure that all information is confidential. Do not include the interviewee's name or other personal information on the written forms. Use a code number instead, such as the identification number for interviewees in the contact log.

4.4.4   Evaluating Cognitive Testing Results

After the interviews are completed, each interviewer summarizes their findings for each question, using an electronic form of the survey questionnaire. All interview notes for each question should then be combined into a comprehensive summary of interviewee comments under each question. This is useful for identifying problems that are reported by multiple interviewees. In addition, each interviewer can provide a general summary of their interpretation of any problems with each survey question.

The summaries are reviewed using qualitative analytic methods, and key problems are identified. This can include coding to identify the main issues among interviewees (Presser and Blair, 1994; Hughes, 2004), as listed below:

Code 1:   Difficulties understanding the meaning of a question or particular words or concepts.
Code 2:   Difficulties remembering information needed to answer a question.
Code 3:   Different understandings of a question across interviewees.
Code 4:   Difficulties formulating or reporting an answer to a question.

It is good practice to discuss findings in detail with everyone who is actively involved in the questionnaire design process, including questionnaire designers who may not have participated in the cognitive interviewing process. The meetings should be used to point out problems and to suggest solutions. For example, whenever a term is not clearly understood, it should be replaced by one that is easier to understand. The evaluation should identify common trends across interviews (problems that appear frequently) and errors that might only have been identified in a single interview, but that could threaten data quality or show up more frequently in the full survey.

After completion of the interviews and analysis of the feedback, the research group can revise the questionnaire according to the interviewees' comments. If it is clear after only a few interviews that there are major problems to be corrected, then the questions should be modified before continuing with the interviews. Especially in the first phase, as few as four interviews may be sufficient to constitute a 'round' of interviews.

Questions fail when one or more interviewees find the question too difficult to answer accurately, do not understand the question as intended, or the interviewees have very different interpretations of the meaning of the question. Failed questions need to be substantially revised and re-tested, but questions that also fail the second or final phase of cognitive testing will need to be discarded.

Major changes to the question or response options will be required if almost all interviewees give the same response, indicating that the question will collect very little information; for instance, almost all interviewees reply 'yes' or 'no' to a nominal question, or select the same response category in an ordinal question. This can be solved for nominal questions by changing them into ordinal questions and re-testing. For ordinal questions, new response categories may be needed. New response options may also be required if interviewees had difficulties reporting an answer because they found none of the options to be relevant or satisfactory.

Minor issues can be addressed through new wording or definitions of the main question or response options to address a lack of understanding, culturally oriented defects or logical flaws.

Other issues that can be identified in cognitive testing include (Willis, 2005):

1. Poor specification of objectives and how questions address them.
2. Poor question order, including unnecessary or confusing repetition and other interactions between survey questions.
3. Overly long or demanding questions.
4. Limitations on what can be asked of survey respondents.

Given the small samples involved in cognitive interviewing, the interviewers' judgement of whether a question succeeded or failed should affect how the question is revised, or not. For example, very idiosyncratic interview results can sometimes be ignored, for instance with an interviewee who has a very restricted vocabulary. However, volunteers for cognitive testing are usually considerably more motivated to carefully think about questions than a sampled population. Decisions on whether to revise or reject a question need to take this into account. What might appear to be a minor issue should not be taken lightly, with an effort made to solve the problem.

4.5   WEB PROBING

An experimental alternative to conducting cognitive testing in person or via a video link is web probing (Behr et al., 2017; Fowler and Willis, 2020; Neuert et al., 2021). A short online version of up to nine questions can be cognitively tested by following each question with a probe that asks for information such as why a specific response was selected out of several options, the respondent's understanding of a term, or for details on what the respondent was thinking when answering a question. The web probe questionnaire should not include more than nine questions because of the high respondent burden from asking open questions (Behr et al., 2017), but survey questions can be divided into multiple short web probe questionnaires. Table 4.4 gives an example of one question and its probe. Questions 1 and 2 should appear on separate screen

Table 4.4   Example of a web probe question

In the last year, did your company introduce new hiring practices to increase staff diversity?	
Yes	☐
No	☐

In the previous question, how did you interpret the term 'staff diversity'?

views so that the second open question does not affect how respondents answer the first question.

Web probing has two advantages over an in-person interview. It can reach a larger number of respondents, providing more data for evaluation, and it eliminates the cost of training and the time required to conduct interviews. Conversely, there are several disadvantages. It can only reach individuals who are online, it does not permit interactive probing of responses, respondents can lack motivation (Meitinger and Behr, 2016), and it is experimental, with most testing on individuals from non-probability online panels that are not representative of managers (Lenzner and Neuert, 2017).

Until there is more evidence for web probing, including of managers, it may be advisable to use in-person interviews. However, web probing can be a useful supplement to interviews by providing results for a larger sample.

4.6   PILOT SURVEY

A pilot survey implements the full questionnaire on a small sample of individuals that are randomly drawn from the population of interest. The number of individuals can vary between 50 and several hundred but should be considerably lower than the planned full survey. If the full survey will only be sent to 500 individuals, a pilot survey sent to between 50 and 75 individuals should be sufficient.

Ideally, the survey method for a pilot survey should match the planned method for the full survey. If the plan is to conduct a postal survey, the pilot survey should ideally be sent by post. However, an online survey can be much faster and, as discussed below, the ability to collect paradata is a major advantage for conducting a pilot survey online. Similarly, to save costs, a planned pilot of a face-to-face interview survey could be conducted by telephone.

Cognitive testing focuses on question comprehension. Instead, the purpose of a pilot survey is to provide useful information on the questionnaire length, flow, ease of response, the location of high termination rates, and data on response options. The pilot test should use a random sample of the same population as the full survey. Do not add pilot survey responses to those of a full survey if the pilot results in any changes to the questionnaire – which is almost always the case.

Information on the questionnaire length can be measured by the time required to answer the questionnaire and if there is a trend to satisficing behaviour or lagging interest for questions placed towards the end of the questionnaire. Time to answer can be collected through paradata for an online version (section 4.6.1 below), but for printed questionnaires the respondents can be asked to record the start and finish times on the questionnaire or asked to estimate the time required to answer. Questionnaires that take too long to complete (more than 15 minutes) should be reduced in length. Options include deleting difficult questions or asking questions using a simpler method (ordinal categories instead of an open interval question), reducing the number of sub-questions in a matrix question, and deleting non-essential questions. Ease of response can be measured through the time taken for each question (only possible through collecting paradata for an online version) and the item non-response rates, with high item non-response a marker for difficult or poorly written questions. Incorrect or implausible answers can also be used as markers of poor questions.

The location of premature termination can be identified on postal question-naires, but only if the respondents return them. For instance a significant per-centage of respondents could respond to a difficult question half-way through the questionnaire through abandoning the remainder of the questionnaire, with all questions after this point left blank. If this occurs, it is very important to identify the problem question or sections and revise as needed.

Pilot test results for binary and ordinal questions can be used to assess the suitability of response options to differentiate between different groups of respondents. If there is insufficient differentiation, the response options will need to be rewritten or the measurement level changed, as discussed above in section 4.4.4.

4.6.1 Paradata From an Online Pilot Survey

Belfo and Sousa (2011) and Fan and Yan (2010) strongly recommend collect-ing paradata on how respondents complete the survey to identify undesirable respondent behaviour such as premature termination or problematic questions. Paradata can help to identify questions that are difficult for respondents to understand – for instance if question response times are considerably longer than the average, if questions are uninteresting or too long, resulting in speeding through the question – or to assess poor usability, such as when respondents go back to check definitions or instructions. If a high percentage of respondents return to an earlier point, it could suggest the need to change the question order, for instance by moving the question where the returns originate to an earlier location in the questionnaire. Alternatively, it may be necessary to repeat definitions or instructions.

If the pilot survey is conducted online, collect the following paradata:

1. The time to answer the full questionnaire.
2. The time spent on answering each question. This is not necessary for the sub-questions within a matrix question, unless there is a reason for thinking that some of the sub-questions will be difficult.
3. Rollover mouse paths which will provide some evidence on what is read carefully, particularly instructions.
4. Click (audit) trails to determine if question answers have been changed or if the respondent returns to earlier pages, for instance to reread questions or definitions.

Audit trail paradata have an additional purpose if the full survey will combine online and postal delivery of printed questionnaires (section 5.7). Good practice suggests 'greying' questions that are skipped in the online version to improve comparability with completing a printed questionnaire. If the audit trails in the pilot survey find that very few respondents changed their answer after viewing 'greyed' questions, it may not be necessary to 'grey' questions for the purpose of maintaining comparability.

4.7   CONCLUSIONS

Problems due to poor data quality or insufficient data can't be corrected through statistical analysis. If the questions are poorly designed, you will continually be haunted by the ghost of 'garbage in garbage out'.

The best method to improve data quality and prevent undesirable respondent behaviour that results in a lack of data due to premature termination or skipping questions is to test the questionnaire. Testing helps to ensure that the data collected by the questions are of high quality, meeting requirements for content validity (the questions measure what the researcher wants to measure), inter-rater validity (questions are interpreted in the same way by different respondents), and reliability (respondents give accurate responses that result in very few false positives and false negatives).

Questionnaires should be first tested on colleagues, followed by cognitive testing with a minimum of ten respondents drawn from the population of interest. Cognitive testing is not perfect, in part because the high cost limits the number of interviews and because volunteers for cognitive testing tend to be more interested in and motivated by the topic covered in the questionnaire than other individuals in the population of interest.

If sufficient funds are available, follow up cognitive testing with a pilot test or web-based probes that provide additional information on questionnaire length, flow, ease of response, questions that cause high termination rates, and data on response options, such as the location of category boundaries. Online pilot surveys should collect paradata on the time spent on specific questions and audit trails to identify problematic questions, definitions and question placement. Pilot testing is particularly useful for identifying problems that reduce the amount of data collected, such as premature termination or speeding through questions, since data collected from speeders may need to be removed before analysis.

5.   Survey implementation

5.1   INTRODUCTION

Survey implementation consists of five activities to collect data from sampled individuals: (1) selecting a survey method, (2) obtaining ethics approval where necessary and meeting confidentiality and open data requirements for making your data publicly available, (3) writing up a protocol to manage the sample selection and questionnaire delivery, (4) selecting individuals to sample, and, finally, (5) delivering the questionnaire. The first four tasks involve preparations before survey delivery and involve a considerable amount of effort, particularly to select and obtain contact information for sampled individuals. The final task of delivering the questionnaire can take several months and much attention to detail, but once underway should proceed smoothly with a small amount of effort.

This chapter describes all five activities. It is not provided in the same order as you may follow in your research because an understanding of the activities to select the sample, to estimate the required sample size and to deliver a survey is required before you can develop your protocol or estimate a budget.

Survey implementation also includes the construction and maintenance of data files for the contact details for sampled individuals and to track questionnaire delivery and returns over time. These data-related activities are covered in section 6.1.

5.2   CHOICE OF SURVEY METHOD

There are four survey methods in common use that match the four types of questionnaires: telephone interviews, face-to-face interviews, a postal survey where printed questionnaires are mailed to sampled individuals, and an online survey. The last method is usually designed to be accessible through a computer, but sampled individuals may also access the questionnaire via a tablet or smartphone.

The process of implementing a survey is similar across the four survey methods, but there are a few notable differences that affect survey costs, including the cost of skilled labour, the time to conduct a survey, and data quality. Importantly, there are also expected differences in response rates. On average, the response rates for online surveys are 11 to 12 percentage points lower than the response rates for other survey methods, even after the use of steps to increase response rates such as mailing an invitation letter and multiple follow-up reminders to non-respondents (Cho et al., 2013; Shih and Fan, 2008; Daikeler et al., 2020). Many sampled individuals could prefer a different survey method to answer the questionnaire or delete email invitations unread, due to concerns over spam (Dillman et al., 2014). Response rates by survey type can also vary by the type of person. Younger individuals and those with extensive experience with information technology are more likely to reply to an online survey than to a mailed survey (Saunders, 2012).

The decision as to which method to select will depend on the amount of funding available, the availability of survey skills, particularly for interviews, and the calendar time required to conduct the survey, or the amount of time that it is 'in the field'. Table 5.1 summarizes the effect of the survey method on costs and skills, data quality and calendar time. The comparison assumes that the two interview methods are conducted using computerized software that the interviewer uses to enter the results into a laptop or tablet and returned postal surveys that use machine readable paper questionnaires. If machine readable questionnaires are not used, for instance to reduce respondent burden, the data entry costs for printed questionnaires switches from moderate to high.

Compared to postal questionnaires where the respondent completes a printed version of the questionnaire, the use of survey software to collect question responses, as in face-to-face, computer assisted telephone interviews (CATI) and online surveys, can improve data quality. For instance, survey software can include automated warnings if percentages do not sum to 100%, if the respondent (or interviewee) provides an answer that is not permitted, or if the respondent does not answer the question. Automated filter and skip instructions reduce respondent burden, which should also improve data quality. In addition, material costs for paper and postage are lower for methods using a computer interface, although they are not eliminated, as the first contact for an online survey should be sent by post.

Table 5.1 indicates that online surveys are the least costly and produce the best data quality of all methods, while face-to-face interview surveys are the most expensive due to high labour costs for employing and training interviewers about the purpose of the questions and avoiding bias. Postal surveys are the most expensive for material costs, but these are usually considerably less than the high labour costs for interview surveys. Face-to-face interviews are the costliest because of the additional time required for interviewers to travel to meet respondents. In addition, the calendar time to conduct a face-to-face survey will vary by the number of trained interviewers and the number of planned interviews. Despite its drawbacks, a face-to-face survey may be required for cultural reasons or for a semi-structured interview format with

Table 5.1   *Cost (C),[a] data quality (DQ), and time (T) advantages of each survey method*

		Heard surveys		Read surveys	
Task		Telephone (CATI) interview	Face-to-face interview	Online	Postal (printed questionnaire)
Automated checks for valid answers	DQ	Yes	Yes	Yes	No
Automated filter and skip instructions	DQ	Yes	Yes	Yes	No
Personalized answers to respondent questions on questionnaire items	DQ	No	Yes	No	No
Material (printing, postage, etc.) costs	C	Low	Moderate	Moderate	High
Telephone costs	C	High	Moderate	Low	Low
Travel costs[b]	C	Nil	High	Nil	Nil
Skilled labour costs	C	High	High	Low	Low
Data entry costs	C	Low	Low	Low	Moderate
Post-survey data cleaning costs	C	Low	Low	Low	Moderate
Time required (start to end) of questionnaire in the field	T	Low[c]	High[e]	Moderate[d]	High[e]

Notes: [a] Per realized response, costs vary by local prices; [b] Excludes travel costs for cognitive testing (see Chapter 4), as this applies to all survey methods. Calendar time ranges: [c] (low): less than one month, given sufficient interviewers; [d] (moderate): one to three months, for online survey method determined by time between successive follow-ups; [e] (high): three to four months, for printed survey method determined by time between successive follow-ups.

multiple open questions. A CATI survey could be appropriate if results are needed quickly and if funds are available to employ sufficient interviewers to complete the survey quickly.

Unless there are good reasons for using interview methods, Table 5.1 indicates that the least expensive method is an online survey in countries where all sampled individuals have internet access and a findable email address. To overcome the disadvantage of online surveys for response rates, National Statistical Offices often provide the choice of an online or postal format and may also collect results through a CATI survey method. Fortunately, with a few exceptions (Grable and Britt, 2011), research has not found significant differences in the quality, reliability, response behaviour or types of results obtained through printed and online surveys (Alvares et al., 2011; Huang, 2006; Leiner, 2019; Weigold et al., 2013), which suggests combining postal and online methods for a voluntary survey.

Compared to a postal-only or online-only survey, a combined postal and online survey, with the postal version coming first, can increase response rates by 10 percentage points (Dillman et al., 2009) for voluntary surveys. The postal/online sequence obtains a slightly higher response rate than the reverse of an online/mailed sequence (Millar and Dillman, 2011), but a lower response rate for an online/mailed sequence may be an acceptable trade-off for lower printing, postage and data entry costs. Following an online survey with a postal option can also be essential if some of the target population is less comfortable with online surveys, for example older or less educated individuals (Kelfve et al., 2020). There is one important caveat: do not offer a choice at the start of the survey, which can confuse sampled individuals and reduce the final response rate by more than 10 percentage points (Medway and Fulton, 2012; Millar and Dillman, 2011).

Respondents can access and complete an online survey on a desktop or laptop, a tablet or a smartphone by clicking on the link in an email. This is an advantage for younger respondents who are more likely than older respondents to use a smartphone to complete a questionnaire (Skeie et al., 2019), but there are two significant disadvantages. First, an analysis of millions of respondents to web surveys finds that the percentage of respondents who completed all questions in a questionnaire is higher for those who answered using a desktop or laptop (83%) versus those who answered on a tablet (66%) or smartphone (63%) (Brosnan et al., 2017). Second, the time required to answer a questionnaire on a smartphone is up to 40% longer than answering the same questionnaire on a desktop or laptop (Skeie et al., 2019; Toninelli and Revilla, 2020). The longer time required to answer on a smartphone is one reason why the completion rate is lower. Longer completion times for smartphones need to be addressed through shorter questionnaires and a reduction in the length of list and matrix questions (section 3.7.2).

Respondents are most likely to use the device on which the invitation letter was read to access the questionnaire and they are unlikely to change to a different device if they find that the process is too slow (Brosnan et al., 2017) or if the questionnaire is not optimized for their device. Unfortunately, you may not be able to control the device used to answer an online questionnaire. Your best option is to use the survey invitation letter to request sampled individuals to complete the questionnaire on a desktop or laptop, or provide the estimated time to complete the questionnaire on a desktop or laptop versus a smartphone. These options may be sufficient for organizational surveys sent to managers and other professionals, but may not be effective for surveys of individuals.

A survey by smartphone could be the best option in conflict zones or in countries where very few people have access to a desktop or laptop. The book edited by Hoogeveen and Pape (2020) (available at no cost online) is a good resource for how to conduct smartphone surveys under these conditions.

5.3   ETHICS APPROVAL AND CONFIDENTIALITY

Questionnaire surveys on the activities of organizations can be subject to supranational, national or institutional rules governing ethics, data confidentiality and open data. The European Union (EU) is a supranational body with laws on data confidentiality that apply in all EU member states, while European-funded research projects need to meet 'open data' rules that encourage access to microdata by other researchers. Universities may require ethics approval, set at a national or institutional level, for research surveys conducted by students or academics, while some academic journals, particularly in the health sciences, require ethics approval to publish research results.

It is important to be aware of the rules and regulations that affect your survey because they may affect implementation, such as the contents of a contact letter and the protection and handling of collected data. Regulations can also affect the questions that you include in your questionnaire. For instance, you may decide to exclude personal questions on the respondent to avoid creating problems with ethics approval or data confidentiality laws. If your survey is funded by the European Commission, you may need to address open data requirements through a survey question that requests permission to make the respondent's anonymized microdata available for use by other academic researchers.

5.3.1   Ethics

Ethics requirements vary by country and type of institution. Universities in many countries have ethics committees that grant ethics approval for health research such as clinical trials and social research on individuals or organizations, while in other countries ethics approval may not be required for research on organizations such as businesses or government agencies. Researchers working for businesses often do not require ethics approval for non-medical research and there may be no ethics committee that they can turn to for advice.

Ethics approval can place limitations on the types of questions that can be asked and the types of people that are included in the sample. You must determine if you need ethics approval before completing the design of your questionnaire. If yes, you may need to provide an ethics committee with information on your survey protocol and submit copies of planned correspondence, such as your contact letter and reminder letters and a preliminary copy of your questionnaire.

There are three ethical concerns relevant to a survey that are discussed below. Even if you do not need the approval of an ethics committee to conduct your survey, you should still follow good practices to ensure that these three ethical concerns are met (Lindorff, 2010). Meeting them should also have a positive effect on the willingness of sampled individuals to complete your questionnaire.

Do no harm to respondents

Ethics approval is often divided into high- and low-risk research, with the demands for high-risk research considerably more stringent than the demands for low-risk research. The separation between high and low risk usually concerns the level of physical or mental risk or discomfort for the study participants. In addition, participation in the study should cause no social or economic risks, such as a loss of the respect of colleagues or income. Therefore, the first ethical objective is to ensure that completing the survey will cause minimal emotional, mental, social or economic harm to the respondent due to asking personally invasive, culturally sensitive or controversial information that might embarrass or upset respondents. This is mostly an issue for social research on individuals. Including sensitive questions or including specific types of individuals in your sample (children, indigenous people, people with disabilities, pregnant women, etc., are included as high risk in some countries) may switch your ethics approval from a low-risk to a high-risk request.

For most research on organizations, only a few personal questions are likely to be relevant and these questions are unlikely to create high risk for respondents. Common questions include the respondent's job level, years of work experience and highest level of education. Research on gender issues in management may require data on the respondent's gender. Other research could need questions that could require high-risk ethics approval, such as research on gender or racial biases in the workplace or research on corruption.

Protect confidentiality and privacy

The second ethical requirement is that the survey meets any concerns that the respondent may have over confidentiality and privacy. This can also be important for reducing social and economic risks. The survey contact letter must offer confidentiality and describe how privacy will be protected. Confidentiality and privacy may also be covered by national or supranational data privacy legislation, as discussed in section 5.3.2 for European Union countries. There may also be ethics approval requirements to ensure that the data are stored securely and the length of time that data must or can be kept. Regulations could specify both a minimum and maximum length of time for storing study data.

Ethics approval in many jurisdictions and the General Data Protection Regulation (GDPR) rules for the collection of personal data in the European Union require data to be collected for a specific and defined purpose (Article 5.1.b in the GDPR), which in the survey context needs to be described in the contact letter. Researchers are not permitted to use data for purposes that were not described in the contact letter, including selling survey data for commercial use.

In some jurisdictions survey respondents have a right to request that their data be deleted after submitting their questionnaire. Some jurisdictions such as Australia require respondents to make such a request within a specified number of months after completing the questionnaire.

Obtain informed consent
The third ethical requirement is to ensure that sampled individuals can make an informed choice on whether to participate. Surveys in the European Union countries are also required to obtain informed consent to meet the GDPR rules for the collection of personal data (Article 4.11). Obtaining informed consent requires giving sampled individuals a description of the research purpose of the survey, the source of funding, the nature and duration of their involvement in the study, how data will be used and stored, who will have access to the data, and how anonymity of the respondent and confidentiality of their data will be maintained. Consent can be obtained by asking the respondent to sign a consent form, which is a simple matter for in-person interviews but impractical for CATI, online and postal surveys. For these, consent can be assumed to be given if the person completes and returns (or verbally answers) the questionnaire. In some jurisdictions the contact letter may need to include a statement on assumed consent.

5.3.2   Confidentiality and Privacy

Confidentiality and privacy rules governing survey research vary substantially from country to country. This section focuses on the European Union General Data Protection Regulation (GDPR) 2016/679[1] because it provides some of the strongest privacy protection in the world. Other countries are likely to have weaker privacy protection, but following the GDPR rules provides a good framework for protecting privacy and confidentiality that should reassure your sampled individuals and improve response rates.

The GDPR was largely introduced to protect individuals from the unwanted use of their data by internet firms such as Google (Alphabet), Amazon and social network companies such as Facebook (Meta), but some of the GDPR regulations apply to data collected by governments or by researchers for scientific research. An overview of the intent of the GDPR states that the regulation is relevant to 'the processing of personal data for … scientific or historical research' and that these types of analyses are 'subject to appropriate safeguards for the rights and freedoms' of individual persons. A major privacy safeguard is that scientific research must ensure that the results of any analyses cannot be used to identify individuals.

If you intend to implement a survey within the European Union, your survey must meet the GDPR survey requirements, even if the survey is conducted from a country outside the European Union.

The GDPR rules are applicable to personal data only, defined as 'any information that relates to an identified or identifiable living individual'. Personal data include contact data required to implement a survey, such as a first and last name, a location and a personal email address. Personal data also include information collected by a questionnaire on the 'physical, physiological, genetic, mental, economic, cultural or social identity' of the respondent (Article 4.1). This includes information on the respondent's age, gender, job level, years of work experience and highest level of education. Personal data do not include respondent answers to questions on their organization, but it is good practice to apply the same rules to all organizational data collected by your survey.

The GDPR definition of personal data encompasses de-identified, encrypted or anonymized data (referred to in the regulation as 'pseudonymised') if analysis of this data can be used to re-identify a person. This means that it applies to data that can be reassembled, for instance if an anonymized database of the survey results contains sufficient information that an interested person could use it to determine a respondent's identity.

The GDPR puts more stringent limits on the processing of sensitive personal data, such as on 'ethnic origin, political opinions, religious or philosophical beliefs, or trade union membership'. Respondents must give specific consent for the analysis of sensitive data (Article 5.9.1).

A final GDPR requirement to keep in mind is that respondents have the right to request information on what personal data are retained or ask for its removal from your dataset (Article 13).

Based on the GDPR, the ethics requirements of several countries and respondent concerns over the confidentiality of their data, good practice requires offering full confidentiality in the contact letter to interviewees or survey respondents. This will also encourage participation. The contact letter that provides informed consent needs to note that:

> No information will be released in any form (oral, printed, online, etc.) that could be used to identify the respondent or their organization.
> Access to the microdata will be restricted to people/organizations that are identified in the contact letter.

For the second point, individuals do not need to be named, but a reference to 'academics within the project research group' or another form of restriction is necessary. Respondents must know that their microdata will not be shared widely.

Offering confidentiality can create problems when regulations or funding rules require the microdata from publicly funded studies to be made publicly available for use by other academics. Anonymization (section 6.3.3) will meet the first requirement because anonymized data cannot be used to identify respondents or their organization, but ethics approval may still require informed consent for the release of anonymized data. If this is the case, consent should not be obtained in the contact letter as this is very likely to reduce responses. Instead, include a final question in your questionnaire that asks respondents, on a yes or no basis, if they agree for their anonymized data to be made publicly available to other academics for non-commercial research only. Data from respondents who report 'no' must be excluded from the anonymized data.

5.4   IMPLEMENTATION PROTOCOL

A protocol is a list of instructions that describe how a survey will be implemented. An example is given in section 4.3 for cognitive testing interviews. There are multiple perspectives on a survey protocol, ranging from complete protocols that cover the purpose of the survey, questionnaire development, implementation, data analysis and the dissemination of the results to protocols that only cover implementation. The description below is limited to survey implementation.

The survey implementation protocol consists of written instructions for how the survey will be conducted and covers the definition of the population of interest, construction of a sampling frame, the sampling method (census, simple random sample, stratified random sample, etc.) and the delivery of the questionnaire to sampled individuals. The latter includes the first contact letter, the timing of follow-up contacts for non-respondents and separate follow-up letters or emails (each one should differ). If a second survey of non-respondents is conducted (section 6.2.2), a separate implementation protocol will be required for it. The protocol is supported by a spreadsheet file that tracks the implementation process over time for all units in the sample (section 6.1).

The purpose of the implementation protocol is to ensure that all necessary steps have been identified to maximize response rates over the time span of the survey implementation. For random samples, the protocol also ensures that all potential respondents have an opportunity to respond to the survey, such that the probability of responding is unbiased. The latter goal is an ideal that is not always met. Researchers may alter the follow-up protocol if the expected response rate for high interest organizations is very low. This could result in extra effort to obtain responses from important organizations. For instance, a survey on the use of biotechnology for industrial processing might give greater effort to obtaining responses from large, dedicated biotechnology firms than from small firms that may or may not use biotechnology.

5.5   SAMPLE SELECTION

Sample selection consists of identifying the target population of interest, constructing a sample frame, selecting individuals to contact for the survey, and deciding on a sampling method.

5.5.1   Target Population

The population of interest consists of all organizations that are relevant for your research questions. The sample frame consists of a list of organizations in your population that are drawn upon to create the sample to be surveyed, while the sample fraction equals the fraction of the sampling frame that you will survey. Ideally, the sample frame equals the target population, but this is often not possible, either because some organizations in the target population are not found, or key data for selection are missing. For instance, the population could include 10,000 organizations, but complete contact data are only available for 9,600, which make up the sample frame. If 1,920 are surveyed, the sample fraction is 0.2 (1,920/9,600).

For surveys of businesses, the best estimate of the entire population is the official business register, maintained by national statistical offices, which contains data on all businesses by size category and industry. In some countries such as the Netherlands academics can purchase business register data, while in other countries official business registers are confidential and not available to researchers. In other jurisdictions business registers can be queried (for all countries within the European Union through the European e-justice website), but it may be difficult to use them to draw a sample. The alternative is to use commercial versions such as Dun and Bradstreet in the United States or Orbis, provided by Bureau van Dijk in Europe. Orbis also provides business register type data for many other countries. Commercial business registers are useable for drawing a sample but may be less up to date than an official business register.

Some public sector organizations are also included in commercial business registers, but there are also separate registers in many countries for government organizations, although they vary by the amount of detail that they provide. As an example, the national government of Australia provides a continuously updated online list of national government organizations.[2] The register includes information on the purpose of the organization, an address and a main telephone number, but it does not provide information on staff. Other governments provide separate lists by type of government organization, such as government corporations or ministries, which requires multiple online searches to identify all organizations.

Some non-profits including non-governmental organizations (NGOs) can be included in commercial business registers but constructing a register of all NGOs in a country or region may need to draw on multiple sources, including lists maintained by government agencies and non-profit associations. Government lists are often produced by individual ministries and list NGOs relevant to the ministry only. As examples, the Australian Department of Foreign Affairs and Trade (DFAT) maintains a list of NGOs active in development programmes[3] while Environment and Climate Change Canada maintains a list of Canadian NGOs active in environmental issues.[4]

In a survey of organizations, the population consists of 'statistical units' that can be a legally defined organization or a subset of an organization, such as a department, division or agency. For businesses, a legally defined organization is the enterprise, which is the smallest, legally defined unit of a business. Business surveys can also cover kind of activity units (KAU) such as manufacturing plants or research laboratories, or they can cover divisions that specialize on specific markets. For example, the Swiss multinational ABB has four main divisions, electrification, process automation, motion, and robotics and automation, that are further sub-divided into specific product lines. Other organizational units of possible interest include universities or their administrative departments and faculties, hospitals or hospital departments, government ministries, agencies or departments, educational establishments such as primary and secondary schools, and households.

A problem that is specific to organizational surveys is that the population can be defined by a set of organizations or work units within organizations but constructing a sampling frame requires the ability to identify individuals within each sampling unit who have the expertise and knowledge to answer the survey questions (Fulton, 2018). Complex organizational structures can make it difficult to identify work units of interest or a qualified individual to answer your questionnaire. Many organizational surveys are best answered by a respondent who is the head of a division or department, but it is very rare to find an existing public directory of all relevant division or departmental heads from which to construct a sampling frame. Instead, researchers often need to build a customized sampling frame that is appropriate for their survey. This is one of the largest and most costly differences between surveys of organizations versus individuals.

For small organizations with fewer than 50 employees, the person in charge (the director, CEO, owner, etc.) is likely to be qualified, through experience and discussions with staff, to answer all questions about their organization, but this is not the case for large organizations. The head of a large organization is likely to be qualified to answer questions on strategy, but unqualified to answer questions on specific activities such as processes to deliver services or challenges that only affect a specific division or work unit within the organization. Conversely, the head of a small unit within a large organization will be knowledgeable about the activities of their unit but may be unqualified to answer questions on corporate strategy.

For a survey of organizations, you need to identify the organizational level for which you want to collect data and the job level or title of individuals who will be qualified to answer your questionnaire. The organizational level can be the entire organization, a department or division, a work unit or even individual employees. The target population must be manageable, either because it is small enough to make a census possible, or because it is possible to construct a sample frame for all eligible units from which to draw a sample.

Example for a public sector survey
To explain these issues, I use an example of a hypothetical study by a researcher on the costs and benefits of contracting out services by public sector organizations. The theoretical population consists of all public sector organizations that contract out services. This will be a very large number and impractical to survey. For most research the population will need to be reduced by a defined set of inclusion and exclusion criteria into a manageable number of statistical units. The first inclusion factor selected by the researcher is location within a specific country. A second factor is restriction to municipal governments only, with national and regional governments excluded. This still leaves thousands of potential organizations, so the researcher adds a third criteria of municipalities with over 10,000 inhabitants, leaving a population of 1,000 municipalities. These exclusion and inclusion criteria will limit the generalizability of the research results, but there may be good reasons for assuming that contracting out in mid- to large-sized municipalities will be similar to contracting out in other government organizations. Furthermore, the set of eligible municipalities is economically and socially significant on its own.

From these municipalities, the researcher needs to identify a target population of potential respondents. One option is to select the elected mayor or the highest civil servant in each municipality, which would give a sample frame of 1,000, one for each municipality. However, the researcher has good reasons to expect that the mayor or highest civil servant will lack the hands-on experience with contracting out services to answer the questionnaire. A better alternative is to contact departmental heads, for which the researcher estimates a population of over 10,000. This is not only too large a population for the researcher's available budget, but wasteful, since many of these departmental heads are likely to have little experience with contracting out. The researcher decides to limit the population to the heads of departments that are involved in services to the public (excluding business and internal services) where contracting out is likely. A search through municipal organization charts identifies five common departments of interest: waste services (garbage, recycling, etc.), water and sewage services, transportation services, housing services, and cultural services. The researcher defines the target population as the departmental heads of up to five citizen-oriented services in municipalities with over 10,000 inhabitants in a specified country. The maximum size of this population is 5,000 (five departmental heads per city), but smaller cities may combine some of these responsibilities, so the researcher estimates that the target population is between 3,000 and 4,000.

The organizational level for this survey is the department, which means that the questionnaire needs to instruct the respondent to answer questions for their department only. The next step is to construct a sample frame by identifying all relevant departments. Using the organizational charts for each municipality, the researcher identifies a population of 3,800 relevant municipal departments that constitute the sample frame. The researcher estimates that a realized sample of 500 respondents is required for statistical analysis (section 5.5.3 below) and assumes that the response rate will be 40%. This requires a sample fraction of 0.33 to obtain approximately 1,250 units. Departments are randomly selected and after selection the contact details for each selected department manager are obtained from a combination of searching municipal websites for contact details and telephone calls.

5.5.2   Sampling Method

There are three choices for sampling: a census, where all units within the sample frame are surveyed; a probability sample, where all sampled individuals have a known non-zero probability of selection (Best and Krueger, 2004); and a non-probability sample, where the probability of selection is unknown.

Census
A census is not a sample because all individuals or organizations that meet defined criteria are selected, with the sample fraction equal to 1.0. For small populations, it is always simpler to implement a questionnaire survey as a census than to take a sample. If possible, reduce your population to a size that can be surveyed as a census. For instance, you may have budgeted for 500 respondents, but your estimated population is 1,000. In this case the addition of one exclusionary variable, for instance a minimum size limit that excludes very small organizations, might be sufficient to reduce your population to 500 units. However, keep in mind that adding inclusion criteria to reduce your population could require a change in your research questions. It may not be

feasible to reduce the population if it eliminates one or more research questions of interest.

The opposite situation is that the size of the population is not much larger than what you can manage, for instance there might be 600 units in the population when you budgeted for a survey of 500. It may be worth the effort to seek additional funding or look for possible cost savings in your planned survey methods, as long as you do not sacrifice cognitive testing.

Probability samples
There are several types of probability samples, including simple, systematic, stratified, and cluster probability samples. Readers who would like more detail on different probability sampling methods should consult Thompson (2012) or other expert sources.

In the example in section 5.5.1 for a study on contracting out services, the sample frame consists of the identifiable target population, from which a sample is drawn. This is a probability sample because the probability of selection for all units in the sample frame is 33%, which is equivalent to a sample fraction of 0.33. As the sample fraction is identical for all sampled individuals, this is also a simple random sample. If the sample frame had been smaller, for instance fewer than 1,000 individuals, it would have been easier to use a census, where everyone in the sample frame is selected.

Probability samples are more costly and demanding than a census because of the additional effort required to build the sample frame. In a census, all statistical units are in the sample frame, but the sample frame for a probability sample includes many statistical units that will not be surveyed. For instance, a probability sample that uses a sample fraction of 0.20 will need to identify five times as many statistical units than sampled units. Basic information on each unit in the sampling frame needs to be obtained. The minimum is the name of the organization, but a stratified sample that uses different sampling frames will also need to collect information on the factor used for stratification, such as the number of employees in the organization (see below). Of note, you do not need to collect contact details for all units in the sample frame. This is only required for sampled units (section 5.6.1 below).

To draw a random sample, list all named units in the sample frame alphabetically or by a different characteristic. Each unit is assigned a sequential number up until the number of units in the population, for instance from 1 to 5,000 in a sample frame with 5,000 units. A random number generator, available in many statistical software packages, can be used to generate a list of random numbers that equals the number of units in the sample frame. The number of selected units depends on the sampling fraction. If the sampling fraction is 0.20, select units out of the 5,000 with a number that matches the first 1,000 randomly generated numbers.

A variant of a simple random sample is a systematic sample. An initial unit is randomly selected. If the sample fraction is 0.20, every fifth unit after the initial unit is selected. The method is more appropriate for individuals because it is difficult to list organizations in a way that does not introduce bias. For instance, it is not a good idea to select every fifth business in an alphabetical list, since the names of businesses can be non-randomly related to their function. In addition, it is a simple matter to select units randomly if they can be listed.

An alternative to a simple random sample is to draw a stratified random sample, with different sampling fractions for two or more strata defined by the characteristics of interest, such as unit size or function. In the example above, the researcher might have drawn a stratified sample for each of the five types of services. This is useful if one or more strata are notably less frequent. For instance, the distribution of service types among the 3,800 units could be as follows: 1,000 for waste, 1,000 for water and sewage, 1,000 for transportation, 600 for housing, and 200 for culture. The lower number of units for housing and culture occurs because these units are only present in larger municipalities. A simple random sample which applies a sample fraction of 0.33 to all strata would sample only 66 cultural units, compared to 333 units for waste, water and transportation services. With an expected response rate of 40%, the estimated realized sample is 26 cultural units, which could be too small to identify significant differences in contracting out between cultural and other types of services (section 5.5.3 below). To solve this problem, the sampling fraction for culture could be increased, for instance to 60%. As the sampling fraction is known, the difference in samples can be taken into consideration for post-survey descriptive analyses (section 7.2.1).

It is common practice in large surveys run by national statistical offices to use multiple sample fractions for different strata, with the sample fraction varying by the number of units in a cell, defined by two or more strata. For instance, the sample frame for businesses often includes strata for industry, region and size measured by the number of employees. Strata by employment usually include tens of thousands of small firms with fewer than ten employees, thousands with between ten and 499 employees, and a few hundred large firms with 500 or more employees. As the economic impact of individual large firms is considerably higher than that of small firms, national statistical offices often use a sampling fraction of 1.0 (a census) for large firms, an intermediate sampling fraction for mid-sized firms (perhaps 0.10) and a smaller sampling fraction for small firms (perhaps 0.02). The sampling fractions can be further adjusted to take account of differences in the number of firms within specific industries and regions.

Cluster sampling is an option that can reduce the costs of constructing a sample frame when the units of interest are located within a common type of organization that is geographically dispersed. An example is departments located within schools, universities, hospitals or municipalities. Instead of constructing a sample frame for all departmental heads in all municipalities, municipalities are randomly selected. In one-stage cluster sampling all departmental heads in sampled municipalities are included in the sample frame, but it is also possible to use a two-stage method where departmental heads are randomly sampled within each randomly selected municipality. Cluster sampling can suffer from higher sampling errors and bias than simple or stratified random samples. If you wish to use cluster sampling, you should consult Thompson (2012) or another expert source to guide the design of your sample.

Non-probability samples
Non-probability samples include convenience, snowball, purposive and quota sampling methods. In these samples the target population is undefined (there is no sample frame) and the probability of an individual unit from the target population being selected for inclusion in the survey is unknown.

A convenience sample occurs when a researcher samples conveniently located individuals or organizations, or those with which the researcher already has contacts. For example, a researcher might survey all school principals located in a ten-kilometre radius.

A snowball sample builds up the number of sampled individuals through connections. The researcher identifies a manager from an organization of interest and then asks that manager for contacts in other similar organizations. Each proposed contact can be asked for additional contacts, with the researcher following the connections until an adequate sample size is obtained.

A purposive or judgemental sample uses expert knowledge, either that of the researcher or of a panel of experts, to select organizations with characteristics or activities of interest. This method is used when the characteristics or activities are rare. For instance, a researcher interested in the use of a novel, advanced manufacturing technology may have evidence that it is only used by less than 0.5% of all manufacturing firms. A random sample would be wasteful, identifying very few of these firms. The alternative is to survey manufacturing firms that experts have identified as very likely to use this novel technology.

A common use of purposive sampling is a survey *of* experts that is addressed to experts on a topic and commonly uses purposive sampling to identify experts. Examples include surveys of identified national experts about their perceptions of a range of topics, such as the ease of doing business or corruption within their country of residence.[5] The disadvantage with this methodology is that the accuracy of the results depends on how the experts are selected, each expert's level of knowledge on the topic, and the factors that influence how expert opinion is formed. The results of these studies can vary over time in response to recent events, suggesting that expert opinion may be influenced by media articles or assumed wisdom.

The main advantage of surveying expert opinions is that it is inexpensive. Otherwise, a description of national, regional or local conditions should be built up by averaging the results of a survey that randomly selects individuals and asks questions limited to each person's own area of expertise. For example, a survey on corruption could ask business managers if they have been affected by corruption, and if yes, the type and degree of effects on their business.

Quota sampling is based on selecting a pre-identified number of organizations or individuals from defined strata. For example, business data could show that 50% of NGOs have fewer than ten employees, 25% have ten to 49 employees, 20% have 50 to 99 employees and 5% have 100 or more employees. The researcher could plan to sample 100 NGOs, using quotas for each size category that matches the known distribution by size: 50, 25, 20 and five NGOs respectively for each size class. A quota sample is a probability sample if random sampling is used and the sampling fraction is known. However, quota sampling is a non-probability sample if a convenience or snowball sample is used to identify organizations or individuals within the strata.

Non-probability samples have two severe disadvantages. First, statistical theory is based on drawing random samples from a population, which means that univariate and bivariate statistical significance tests should not be applied to a non-probability sample. Second, non-probability samples are highly likely to be biased in one or more ways, such that estimates from a non-probability sample do not reflect the real value and cannot be generalized to represent the population (Cornesse et al., 2020; Szolnoki and Hoffmann, 2013).

Non-probability samples, often derived from online surveys, are commonly used to estimate voting intentions or individual preferences by adjusting the sample to match the population of interest. The adjustments can include care in constructing the sample and analytical steps to correct for differences between the sample and the population, such as weighting the sample so that the distribution of individuals by identified characteristics such as age, income, gender and location matches census data. Another method is propensity score weighting (Best and Krueger, 2004). Even after adjustment, online surveys can fail to produce accurate results.

Research on the accuracy of probability and non-probability samples finds that probability samples, including those with low response rates, consistently outperform the accuracy of univariate estimates from adjusted non-probability samples (Cornesse et al., 2020). Non-probability quota samples of businesses could be adjusted after the survey by using a business register to adjust the results by size, sector, location and other variables, but this research suggests that the results will be less accurate than those obtained from a probability sample.

There are several conditions where a non-probability sample can be useful. Cognitive testing should use a purposive sample to identify a variety of interviewees because random sampling would be less efficient when the goal is to obtain a small number (ten to 30) of individuals representing organizational units with very different characteristics (section 4.2.2). A purposive sample, drawing on expert knowledge, may also be advisable when an activity or phenomena of interest is rare. Under good conditions, a purposive sample can approach a census if almost all organizations using a rare activity in a defined region are identified. Non-probability samples can also produce useful results when the opposite occurs – an activity is near universally used. In this case it may be reasonable to assume that the sampling method has a minor effect on drawing inferences on the factors that affect the activity.

Snowball and convenience sampling may be necessary for informal organizations or businesses that are not captured in business registers or for individuals for whom there are no contact details such as a telephone number or a permanent address. For both, the best sampling method may be a combination of a convenience and snowball sample. For instance, a survey of homeless people could visit locations where the homeless tend to congregate and ask homeless individuals for suggestions on where to find additional homeless people. The same approach could also be used for a survey of informal businesses.

5.5.3 Estimating the Minimum Sample Size

The size of a random sample is often determined by the amount of available funding, but a sample that is too small can raise ethical concerns, for instance if a sample is too small to detect meaningful differences between a treatment and a control group. Conversely, a sample that is too large can waste resources and identify results that are statistically significant but meaningless in practice. The minimum optimal sample size refers to realized responses and not to the number of sampled units. For example, with an expected response rate of 40% and a required sample of 500 cases, the sample frame would need to include 1,250 units.

The examples given below require some familiarity with statistics. Fortunately, if you have limited statistical experience, online resources are available for estimating the minimum sample size for you. You only need to enter three or four variables, depending on the type of analysis, into an online estimator.

There are three common uses for survey data, each of which requires a different method to calculate the minimum sample size:

- Univariate or point estimates for the prevalence of a factor in a population, such as voting intentions or the percentage of NGOs that receive government funding.
- Comparing differences in a variable between two groups (bivariate statistics), such as between treatment and control groups, the percentage of large and small businesses that obtain government funding, or the opinions of junior and middle managers on whether senior management creates a supportive environment in their organization.
- Multivariate regression analysis which evaluates the effects of multiple predictor variables on a dependent variable.

Univariate estimates

The sample size for univariate estimates depends on (1) the desired statistical confidence level, such as 0.05, (2) the expected proportion of the population with the characteristic of interest, (3) the acceptable margin of error, and (4) the size of the population. The equation for the minimum sample size for large populations (well over 5,000) is $n = [z^2 * p(1-p)]/e^2$, where z equals the z-score for the level of confidence, p equals the proportion of the population with the characteristic and e equals the acceptable margin of error. For a confidence value of 0.05, $z = 1.96$. The value of p is often unknown and set to 0.5, which maximizes the possible sample size, and e is frequently set at plus or minus 3%. At these values, the minimum sample size is 1,068, but if the margin of error is relaxed to 5% the sample size is 385.

If the purpose of the survey is to produce univariate estimates of the population value of variables for subgroups, the sample size needs to increase so that equivalent samples are obtained for each subgroup. For example, if univariate estimates are required for both male and female managers at a margin of error of 5%, the sample would need to obtain responses from 385 female and 385 male managers.

Online calculators are available for calculating the minimum sample size for univariate estimates – simply search for 'how large a sample is needed?'.

Comparing differences

The sample size for differences between two equal sized groups within the same sample depends on (1) the confidence level, (2) the desired probability or power of not making a type 2 error (accepting a null hypothesis that is false), (3) the effect size, and (4) the lowest prevalence of the characteristic of interest in one of the two groups. The necessary sample size will increase with the confidence level, the desired power, a smaller effect size, and a higher value for the lowest prevalence in one group. For instance, the minimum sample size will increase as the prevalence in one group approaches 50%. In addition, the sample size will need to be increased if the two groups are not of equal size by approximately 20% if one group has twice the share of the sample than the other group (for instance 2/3 versus 1/3) and by 30% if one group has three times the share of the sample than the other group (for instance 3/4 versus 1/4).

An estimate of the effect size depends on the 'meaningful difference' between the two groups, which depends on the goals of the research. A study could be established to evaluate the effect of a programme to increase the number of disadvantaged students attending elite universities. Before determining the size of the sample, the researchers need to decide what would count as a successful programme outcome – for instance an increase in 10%, 20% or 50% in the number of disadvantaged students admitted to elite universities? Given the cost of the programme, the researchers could decide that 20% is the minimum increase (the effect size) that could be considered as a successful outcome. The effect size has a large impact on the required sample size, with a low effect size requiring a much larger sample than a medium or large effect size (for instance a 20% difference versus a 40% or 60% difference).

For an effect size of 15% or larger, a sample of approximately 500 or fewer is usually sufficient for a power of 95% and for all prevalence rates for equal sized groups, while a sample of 700 would be sufficient for the same settings and a fourfold disparity in the share of the two groups in the sample. More details can be found in table 1.3 of Conroy (2018), but remember to double the sample size (which is given for each of two groups in Conroy's table 1.3). Sample size calculators for comparing differences between two groups can be found online by searching for 'sample size for comparing two means'. The online site Medcalc is useful if the number of cases in the two groups differs, but it requires an estimate of the standard deviation for the variable of interest in each group.

Multivariate analyses
The minimum sample size for regression is fortunately smaller than the required size for univariate statistics or for comparing differences between two groups. It varies by (1) the statistical confidence level (p value), (2) the desired power level, (3) the effect size, and (4) the number of predictors, which includes all control and independent variables. With a desired power of 95%, a medium effect size of 40%, a confidence level of 0.05, and three predictors, the minimum sample size is 112. Increasing the number of predictors to ten results in a sample size of 162. The effect size has the largest impact on sample size. With ten predictors, decreasing the effect size from 40% to 20% more than quadruples the required sample size to 619 cases. Sample size calculators

for regression and for ANOVA can be found online by searching for 'sample size regression'.

5.6   QUESTIONNAIRE DELIVERY

Survey delivery requires obtaining contact details for sampled individuals, an initial contact by post or email, and a follow-up routine.

An important factor for increasing participation is to personalize all contacts and to convince everyone in the sample that the survey is of value and their response is important to you. Personalization applies to the initial contact, reminders and follow-up queries over incomplete responses and it applies to contacts by post, email or telephone (Dillman, 2000; Fulton, 2018; Sauermann and Roach, 2013). Establishing the value of the survey is supported by personalization and the effort expended to obtain responses. A survey with no follow-up emails or posted letters sends a signal to sampled individuals that their contribution is of little value to you.

If printed questionnaires are used, either in a postal survey or a combined online/postal survey, the questionnaire should be printed on coloured paper of a light shade, such as light blue, green or pink. The reason for this is that the questionnaire will be more noticeable on the person's desk or among their papers. You can also refer to the questionnaire colour in follow-up reminders.

5.6.1   Contact Details

Contact details are required for all sampled statistical units. An essential step is to address all correspondence to a named individual, including their title within the organization, such as 'Ms Julia Sorrento, Director of Engineering', or 'Dr Rene Kemp, Communications officer'. The inclusion of first names only, last names only, or first and last names in a letter or email will depend on national practice. A randomized survey of PhD students in the United States found that using first names in the contact letter increased response rates (Sauermann and Roach, 2013), but this is probably not the case for corporate managers. With rare exceptions, do not send a questionnaire to an unknown person such as 'Director of Engineering'. Recipients will assume that your contact is junk mail or spam, resulting in a drastic decline in the probability of their replying and very low response rates. This issue is so serious for surveys of managers that it is simply not worth the effort of conducting a survey if you are unable to identify the names for most of your sample. If you can't obtain contact details for named individuals, you should abandon plans to conduct a survey and search for other data sources.

Other contact details can vary by the survey method, but for all survey types it is useful to have a telephone number, an email address and a postal address for all individuals in your sample. In many situations it is a challenge to obtain contact details for sampled individuals from public sources, requiring online research or telephone calls to the relevant organization. Online research may provide names for businesses, public sector organizations and NGOs. Names are also available for some job positions for businesses on commercial databases, but these names are often out of date and will need to be checked through a phone call to the organization.

5.6.2   Initial Contact

Whenever possible, the first contact letter for all survey methods should be sent by post as a postal letter increases response rates over a contact letter by email (Dykema et al., 2012; Daikeler et al., 2020). Email requests to participate face challenges due to spam filters and a well-deserved suspicion of unsolicited emails that may be malicious, such as phishing emails with embedded viruses in attachments (Best and Krueger, 2004; Daikeler et al., 2020). All letters and envelopes should include the logo of your organization, such as a university, business or government logo.

The appearance of the mailing envelope and the letter should be personalized as much as possible so that it does not appear to be part of a mass mail-out of junk mail. Where feasible, this includes using a first-class stamp on the envelope instead of machine franking, handwriting the address instead of using printed labels and signing the invitation letter by hand.

Annex 5.1 provides an example of a basic contact letter. The letter should provide the following information (Fulton, 2018), preferably on a single page (do not go below a 10-point font size):

1. The logo of the organization requesting the data, such as a university logo or an organizational logo. If you can obtain the support of a relevant professional organization, also include their logo and a signature from a high-level official of the organization.
2. A motivation for why the person should participate by completing the questionnaire. This includes explaining the purpose of the study (what the data will be used for).
3. (Optional) Why the person or their organization was selected, for instance it could be random selection or expected expertise on a topic.
4. A promise of confidentiality including a statement that no information will be released, in any form, that could be used to identify yourself or your organization. If you plan to publish results, the promise should state that only aggregated, anonymous information will be released. Depending on ethics requirements, you may need to state when the data will be destroyed.

5. If the survey will be by telephone or face-to-face, give instructions on when they will be contacted to set up an interview. For an online survey, inform selected individuals that they will receive an email invitation within several days with a specified subject line, such as 'Research project on contracting', so that they will be able to recognize the email and differentiate it from spam or phishing emails.
6. An estimate of how long it will take to complete the survey, adjusted for the survey method.
7. A statement that participation is voluntary. If necessary to meet informed consent, add a sentence stating that completing and returning the questionnaire will be assumed to provide consent to the use of the data for the purposes described in the letter.
8. The benefits of participation. This can include the influence of the study on policies of relevance to the individual or their organization and a personal benefit to them, such as the receipt of a study report on completion or a financial incentive.
9. Contact information on who to contact if they have any questions.
10. If required for ethics approval, a footnote giving the ethics reference number and their right to change their mind or opt out of the survey.

The first contact letter for an online survey should be followed a few days later by an email containing a web link to the questionnaire and a unique access password. The password should not include ambiguous letters or numbers such as the letter 'l' and the number '1', or the letter 'o' and the number '0'. The sending address of the follow-up email should be the same as the email address used to send the contact letter and must be from an organization such as a university or business. Do not send emails from a gmail or similar account.

For postal surveys, the contact letter should include the questionnaire and a prepaid reply envelope. Prepaid envelopes of different sizes can be purchased from a post office in almost all countries and are available for both domestic and international mail. Their major advantage is that the respondent does not need to affix a stamp and postage is only paid by the sender (you) if the envelope is used. Make sure that you select an envelope size that is large enough to hold the questionnaire with no more than one fold.

Incentives
There are two common incentives. The first is a report on the results for respondents (section 6.3.5), which takes time to prepare and therefore will incur a cost, even if sent by email instead of by post. The second is a small financial incentive that respondents will receive after completing and returning the questionnaire. A financial incentive is known to increase response rates, although the effect varies by the targeted population (Cho et al., 2013;

Sauermann and Roach, 2013). An incentive can consist of a low-value gift certificate (€15 or $20), for instance to Amazon or another online retailer, or a chance to win one of several larger prizes, such as a €100 or $200 gift certificate. A low chance of a draw on several large prizes is more effective than a high chance of winning a smaller prize, in part because respondents do not know the probability of winning. You can set the total cost of prizes to be equivalent to the personnel cost of preparing and distributing a respondent report. Depending on the length of the questionnaire, a respondent report could take between one and three weeks to prepare.

A concern with financial incentives is that they might encourage replies from unmotivated respondents who engage in satisficing behaviour that lowers the quality of their data. The literature on this is ambiguous, with no effect, a slight improvement in data quality (Cole et al., 2015) and a decline in data quality with financial incentives (Barge and Gehlbach, 2012). Any increase in satisficing behaviours from financial incentives can be addressed in post-survey analyses to identify satisficing and exclude affected cases as needed (section 6.2.3).

5.6.3 Follow-up

Follow-up consists of reminders for non-respondents to complete the questionnaire. The follow-up protocol establishes the number of reminders, the length of time between reminders, the time of day or the day of the week when questionnaires will be distributed or sampled individuals contacted, and the method of contacting them. Reminders also need to be personalized by changing the content of each consecutive reminder letter or email (Sauermann and Roach, 2013). Annex 5.2 contains examples of a first and second reminder.

If only a few staff are available, surveys for more than several hundred individuals may require a staggered mail-out of the postal contact letter over several days. All correspondence by post (contact and follow-up letters) will require several days to arrive, with the average number of days for delivery depending on the country and varying between first- and second-class postage rates. Allow additional time for delays in postal deliveries due to weekends or public holidays. For instance, if post normally takes four working days, a first mail-out of a staggered set of initial contact letters sent on a Monday morning should arrive on the Thursday or Friday of the same week, but a second set of contact letters sent on a Wednesday will not arrive until the following Monday or Tuesday.

The same follow-up protocol should be used for all sampled individuals, with similar gaps between the initial contact letter and each subsequent reminder. It is important to record the mail-out date for each wave of correspondence, so that the follow-up uses the same pattern, such as sending a first reminder

Table 5.2   *Examples of delivery and follow-up protocols by survey method (in days from mailing first contact letter)*

Day	Postal only	Online only	Online/postal	Postal/online
0	Mailed contact letter with printed questionnaire	Mailed contact letter	Mailed contact letter	Mailed contact letter with printed questionnaire
5–7*	-	Email + link to questionnaire	Email + link to questionnaire	-
21	First reminder by post	First reminder email + link to questionnaire	First reminder email + link to questionnaire	First reminder by post
28		Second reminder email + link to questionnaire	Second reminder email + link to questionnaire	
35	Second reminder by post + printed questionnaire			Second reminder by post + printed questionnaire
42		Third reminder email + link to questionnaire	Third reminder by post + printed questionnaire	
49	Third reminder letter by post	Telephone reminder – post printed copy if needed	Fourth reminder by email	Third reminder by email + link to online questionnaire
63	Telephone reminder – post another printed copy if needed		Telephone reminder – post another printed copy if needed	Fourth reminder by email
70				Telephone reminder – post another printed copy if needed

Note: *Allow time for postal delivery plus 2–3 days.

email for an online survey two weeks after you expect sampled individuals to receive the mailed letter. The timing of additional follow-up reminders should maintain similar time gaps between each wave of a staggered mail-out.

Factors such as the timing of a reminder (time of day or day of the week) and the number of days between reminders are unlikely to influence final response rates for an online survey (Sauermann and Roach, 2013). The time of day for contacting sampled individuals will matter for interview surveys. The best strategy is to stagger the first contact and follow-up calls at different times of the day, as some individuals may tend to busy in the morning but available in the afternoon, or vice versa.

Table 5.2 provides examples of delivery/follow-up protocols for postal-only, online-only, online/postal, and postal/online survey methods. These examples can be altered depending on your budget and time constraints.

The effectiveness of reminders is highest for the first and second reminders (Crawford et al., 2001), which should result in a marked increase in the number of questionnaires returned. A third reminder by email will result in additional responses, but at a lower rate, except when it is the first use of the second method in a combined survey. For instance, a third reminder by post that includes the printed questionnaire in a combined online/postal survey will increase the number of responses because it partially 'resets' the survey after two email reminders. Consequently, it is worth following the third reminder by post for a combined online/printed survey with a fourth reminder by email, as shown in Table 5.2 for an 'online/postal' delivery protocol. The same principle applies to combined postal/online surveys.

The examples of implementation protocols in Table 5.2 include a telephone reminder as a final step. Although expensive, these can be very effective depending on the person who makes the reminder calls. This person needs to be personable and capable of reaching potential respondents. Several calls may be required to contact each non-respondent.

At any point in the follow-up, sampled individuals may contact you by telephone, letter or email to request that you stop sending further reminders. You must comply, but by telephone you can ask for a reason if one is not given and gently attempt to convert a refusal into a response. The person might state that they are not eligible to reply, but it is worth checking to ensure that this is true. If yes, remove the case from the sample and record the reason. Asking for the reason for not replying can also identify aspects of the contact letter or questionnaire that were annoying or unclear. If these features are caught early, it may be worthwhile making changes to correct them.

Protocol for CATI and face-to-face surveys
The protocol for surveys conducted through interviews differs because they do not require follow-up reminders. An example protocol is as follows:

1. The first contact letter is mailed out and includes an approximate date for when individuals will be contacted by telephone. If only a few interviewers are available to conduct the interviews, stagger the first contact letters into separate waves to ensure that there are always sufficient interviewers.
2. At the first telephone contact with the sampled individual, the interviewer should refer to the contact letter and briefly describe the purpose of the

questionnaire, the level of confidentiality provided and the time required, and ask if they agree to participate in the survey.

3. For a CATI survey, the interview should be conducted during the first contact call if possible. If not, the interviewer should ask the person for a time that would be suitable for them and make sure that the potential respondent has an email address or telephone number that they can use to change the date and time if necessary.

4. The interviewer contacts the potential respondent at the agreed time to conduct the interview. If the agreed time is more than a few days in the future, the interviewer should send a reminder by email.

5.7   COLLECTING PARADATA FOR THE MAIN SURVEY

Online surveys provide an opportunity to collect paradata on how respondents completed the questionnaire, in addition to its use in online pilot surveys (section 4.6). Paradata collected in the main survey can be used in post-survey analyses (section 6.3.5) to identify unwanted behaviours such as speeding and satisficing that can reduce data quality (Kunz and Hadler, 2020).

Currently, paradata is usually analysed without informing potential respondents, due to concerns that advance notification might reduce response rates and justified by the fact that the analysis of paradata has no value other than testing for data quality. Similarly, respondents to a questionnaire sent by post are not informed that their data will be analysed to identify outliers or missing values (section 6.3). One study found that over 93% of sampled individuals, when asked, agreed to the use of paradata, with little difference if the question for permission was located at the start or end of the survey (Kunz and Hadler, 2020). However, this study used a self-selected panel who were financially motivated to reply to the questionnaire and consequently the results may not be applicable to a voluntary (unpaid) set of respondents. Unless required by an ethics committee, it is up to you to decide whether to mention the use of paradata.

5.8   CONCLUSIONS

Survey implementation requires careful preparation, attention to detail and a clear understanding of the research questions, which determine the population of interest and the estimated realized sample size. The necessary activities to construct a sample frame and to obtain contact information for all individuals in the sample often require more effort than survey delivery. The necessary steps for implementation are also expensive, usually accounting for over half of total survey costs. It may be possible to reduce some costs, but care must be taken to ensure that any steps to reduce costs do not negatively affect the response rate or the quality of the data.

Many of the methods discussed in this chapter will vary by the type of research and available funding, such as the survey method, the definition of the target population, the sampling frame, the type of probability sample used and the sample size. Conversely, the following seven actions are strongly recommended for all surveys:

1. Determine the ethics, confidentiality and open access regulations that you must meet before you start all other implementation steps, since these regulations can affect other decisions.
2. If you hire additional staff, ensure they are sufficiently trained and have an overview of the entire implementation process and their role in it.
3. Use a probability sample, unless you can justify a non-probability sample.
4. Send the first contact letter by post.
5. Send the contact letter and all follow-up reminders to a named individual.
6. Follow up non-respondents and change the wording of each reminder follow-up email or letter.
7. Allow sufficient time, particularly for building a sample frame and for survey delivery.

NOTES

1. The full GDPR regulation and other related information is available at https:// gdpr.eu/
2. https://www.directory.gov.au/reports/australian-government-organisations -register
3. https://www.dfat.gov.au/development/who-we-work-with/ngos/list-of -australian-accredited-non-government-organisations
4. https://www.canada.ca/en/environment-climate-change/corporate/transparency/ briefing-materials/corporate-book/non-governmental-organizations.html
5. Transparency International uses a mix of expert surveys and other data sources to produce a corruption index for multiple countries: https://www.transparency.org/ en/cpi/2021

6. Data processing activities

Data processing is required before analysis and includes processing activities to support data collection and post-survey activities including calculating response rates, non-respondent analysis and data editing (cleaning). There are also several miscellaneous other tasks such as linking survey data to other data sources, anonymization and validation.

6.1   DATA COLLECTION

Data collection includes preparing and maintaining a contact file and a follow-up file, usually in a spreadsheet format, to keep track of contacts and the management of returned questionnaires. Other tasks include question coding, data entry for returned printed questionnaires and checking returned questionnaires for missing data or premature termination.

6.1.1   Data Collection Files

Contact file
A contact file is required that contains the name, job position (Director, Manager, etc.) and contact details of all individuals who will be sent the questionnaire or interviewed. Every individual needs a unique identification (ID) number that is included in the follow-up file (see below), and on printed questionnaires and all data files containing the survey results. The ID number is necessary on the data file in case the respondent needs to be contacted to check the accuracy of a response. The ID number can be a simple number sequence, for instance starting from 001 and continuing to 999 if there are fewer than 1,000 individuals in the sample. The ID number can also include one or more letters, such as letters to identify the contact's country or region.

Contact details to collect will vary by the survey method. A postal-only survey will require a postal address and possibly a telephone number for follow-up, while an online-only survey requires an email address and possibly a telephone number for follow-up. A combined postal and online survey requires both a postal and an email address and possibly a telephone number. It is imperative that the contact file is kept in a secure place, such as a password-protected computer and that electronic or printed back-ups are kept in a locked location. Contact details should not be included in the results data file.

Follow-up file

A follow-up file contains all information of relevance to the implementation of the survey, such as the dates of the first contact, reminders, returns and refusals. This file may include the contact details and the ID number or only the ID number. Figure 6.1 provides an excerpt of a follow-up file for a postal/online survey that does not show the contact information. Eight sampled individuals in the excerpt returned the questionnaire and four did not, of which one sent a refusal to participate after the first email reminder.

The follow-up file needs to include the date that each mail-out or reminder is sent, as this may differ if the mail-outs are sent out in several waves, and the date that the questionnaire was received by you. Once the questionnaire is received, the record in Figure 6.1 shows that the individual was no longer sent further reminders. An additional column notes if a sampled individual refused participation through an email, letter or telephone call. If this occurs, the person should not be contacted again. This is shown in Figure 6.1 for the individual with a QID number of DS012, who is not sent the second email reminder. Some questionnaires may be returned before a reminder can be cancelled. This is shown for case DS001 who sent a postal reply that did not arrive until two days after the first online contact.

The variable 'response received' is coded as 0 = no response, 1 = response received and 2 = refusal. This permits sorting on this variable to identify individuals who need to be sent each of the reminders.

QID	First mailout	Postal Reminder 1	Reminder 2 + questionnaire	First online contact	Reminder 1	Email Reminder 2	Response Received	Date Received	Return format	Date refusal
DS001	01-Mar	15-Mar	30-Mar	15-Apr			1	17-Apr	Post	
DS002	01-Mar						1	06-Mar	Post	
DS003	01-Mar	15-Mar					1	21-Mar	Post	
DS004	01-Mar	15-Mar	30-Mar	15-Apr	25-Apr		1	01-May	Online	
DS005	01-Mar	15-Mar	30-Mar	15-Apr			1	23-Apr	Online	
DS006	01-Mar	15-Mar	30-Mar	15-Apr	25-Apr	05-May	0			
DS007	01-Mar	15-Mar	30-Mar	15-Apr	25-Apr	05-May	0			
DS008	01-Mar	15-Mar					1	28-Mar	Post	
DS009	01-Mar						1	11-Mar	Post	
DS010	01-Mar	15-Mar	30-Mar	15-Apr	25-Apr	05-May	0			
DS011	01-Mar	15-Mar					1	23-Mar	Post	
DS012	01-Mar	15-Mar	30-Mar	15-Apr	25-Apr		2			26-Apr

Figure 6.1   *Extract from a follow-up spreadsheet for a postal/online survey*

Follow-up files are simpler for interview surveys because they only need to include the date of each telephone contact, a response received variable and the date of the completed interview.

Keeping track of the date a questionnaire is received is worthwhile because it may be necessary to include a variable for early and late responders in the results data file. Late respondents may have different characteristics from early responders that affect the results, requiring the inclusion of this variable for late respondents in statistical analyses. Alternatively, late respondents could provide lower-quality data. For surveys that use more than one implementation method, it is also advisable to include a variable in the data file for the method used to respond, for instance if a printed questionnaire was returned by post or if an online version was completed. There may be small differences in replies by post or online that may need to be accounted for in the analyses.

6.1.2   Questionnaire Coding and Data Entry

Before the questionnaire is distributed for all survey methods, the variable name and coding of the responses for each question should be determined. This is necessary for both interview and online versions as it determines the variable names and numeric values that are automatically entered into the data capture software for each question. Select variable names that can be managed by the statistical software that you will use to analyse the data. Survey software can automatically create variable names using the question, but this can produce very long variable names that can be shortened during data cleaning.

The coding for structured questionnaires generally uses integers. For example, questions where only a yes or no response are possible can be coded as 'yes' equals 1 and 'no' equals 0. A three-point importance scale could be coded as 1 for low importance, 2 for moderate importance and 3 for high importance. Coding requires consistency for values that will be used in multiple questions. The value of a 'Don't know' response should be the same for all questions, including 'yes/no' questions and ordinal questions. To avoid conflicts with other question coding, the value of 'Don't know' is often set to equal 9. Similarly, missing values to a question can be given a code such as –99. The negative sign prevents confusion with a real value for use in analysis and will be quickly identifiable in many analyses, such as a frequency distribution.

Data entry
Software programs for interview and online survey methods enter responses directly into a data file. Printed questionnaires that are returned by mail can be formatted to be machine read through automated data entry systems, such as optical character recognition (OCR). OCR services are provided by companies

or may be available at universities. They may require specific markings on the printed questionnaire, which will require formatting the questionnaires before they are printed. Do not use optical mark recognition (OMR) forms that require respondents to mark their answers on a separate page (as for many exams in schools or universities) as this will substantially increase respondent burden.

Alternatively, the responses in printed questionnaires can be manually entered into a data file.

The use of spreadsheet functions such as the form function in Excel can be used to enter data from a printed questionnaire into a spreadsheet, but you will quickly reach a point where it is less time-consuming to use other data entry software that provides a page that looks exactly like each of the printed pages in the questionnaire. In this case, the data entry person only needs to click on the appropriate box or circle that was checked on the printed form. The simplest solution is to use online survey software such as Qualtrics or Survey Monkey to construct the questionnaire for data entry, even if an online version will not be used for the survey. Data for printed questionnaires returned by post can then be entered by staff using the online format.

If multiple survey methods are used, include a variable that identifies each type of questionnaire and its data entry method: printed questionnaires that are manually entered into the software, printed questionnaires that were read by machine, and different online methods where data entry is automated (desktop/ laptop, tablet, smartphone, CATI, face-to-face interviews).

6.1.3 Checking Returned Questionnaires

Questionnaires returned online or by post should be checked as soon as possible for missing data and to determine if the questionnaire was fully completed or if the respondent dropped out before the end (premature termination). When data are missing for a key question, it may be worth contacting the respondent by email to ask if they would complete the question. The email should include the question itself – respondents cannot be expected to remember a question or make an addition or correction in the online version.

Very serious problems in returned questionnaires, for instance if they occur early in the questionnaire or affect a high percentage of respondents, may require mid-survey revisions. A revision should only be made if it can maintain comparability with earlier responses to the questionnaire. For instance, it may be possible to rewrite an interval level question as an ordinal question (earlier responses can be recoded to fit the ordinal question) or use fewer categories in an ordinal question that overlap with the original categories.

Printed questionnaires should be entered into the database as soon as possible so that the results can be checked and for security. (This may incur a cost if the task of machine reading questionnaires is contracted out.) Once the data are entered, the completed questionnaires must be kept in a secure location (section 6.3.2 below).

6.2   POST-SURVEY ACTIVITIES

6.2.1   Calculating Response Rates

Once the survey is completed (no longer in the field), the response rate needs to be calculated. Two response rates are needed: (1) the crude response rate which equals the number of returned questionnaires divided by the number of questionnaires sent out, and (2) the adjusted response rate. The latter adjusts for non-contacts and ineligible responses.

Non-contacts
A failure to contact sampled individuals in a postal or online survey can occur because of an incorrect email or postal address or if the sampled individual is no longer employed in the organization. Errors by post are visible when the package with the questionnaire is returned unopened and errors by email are identified through undeliverable emails. The adjusted response rate equals the number of returned questionnaires divided by the number of questionnaires sent out, minus sampled individuals for whom contact could not be made. For example, if 500 questionnaires were sent out and 200 were returned, the crude response rate is 200/500 or 0.40 (40%). If there were 48 non-contacts the adjusted response rate is 200/(500–48) or 0.442 (44.2%). The adjusted response rate is often several percentage points higher than the crude response rate.

Ineligible responses
The identification of the population and the sampling frame determines eligibility for inclusion in the survey, with questionnaires presumably only sent to eligible individuals. Nevertheless, it is common to receive a few ineligible responses. For instance, the sampling frame could be limited to publicly owned organizations with ten or more employees, but there may be a few responses from private sector organizations or public sector organizations with fewer than ten employees. This occurs because the data used to construct the sampling frame is imperfect or out of date. It is a good idea to include a few questions in the survey to establish eligibility and use this information to identify ineligible responses. Any ineligible responses need to be removed from the numerator, the denominator and the dataset. In the example above, adding five ineligible responses gives an adjusted response rate of 43.6% or 0.436 (200–5)/(500–48–5).

If a simple random sample was used, only the adjusted response rate for all sampled individuals is required. For a stratified random sample, the response rate should also be calculated for each cell within the sampling frame. This will be required for calculating weights for data analysis (section 7.2.1).

6.2.2   Non-respondent Analyses

Non-respondents can differ from respondents in ways that could bias analyses. The next step is to determine which of three types of non-respondent analyses are required:

1. Use existing data to look for differences between the respondents and non-respondents. Existing data can include information used to select the sample, such as the sector and size of the organization, or the job position of sampled individuals. Other information that may be available is the location of all sampled individuals (country, state, region, municipality, etc.) using street addresses or other information, and ownership status (public, private, government, etc.).
2. Compare differences in key variables in the questionnaire between early and late respondents.
3. Conduct a short non-respondent survey.

A simple rule of thumb can be used to determine if non-respondent analysis is required and, if yes, which type is necessary, using the adjusted response rate:

*   80% or greater: no non-respondent analysis is required.
*   50% to 80%: determine if there are significant differences between your respondents and non-respondents using existing data *and* compare early and late respondents.
*   Less than 50%: analyse existing data, compare early and late respondents, and conduct a non-respondent survey if possible.

If a stratified sample was used, it is useful to examine the response rate for each sample cell in the sampling frame and follow the rules of thumb for each sample cell.

Using existing data

Table 6.1 provides an example of a simple random survey of businesses that was conducted at a regional level in 2016. Following the rule of thumb above, this required using existing data to look for differences between the respondents and non-respondents, but a non-respondent survey is not required. Table 6.1 provides existing information on the sector of each case for the full sample (column c) and for respondents only (column a) and non-respondents only (column b). There is little difference in the distribution of sectors between the respondents and the full sample, as shown by comparing the results in columns a and c, but this is because column c includes the cases in column a. A comparison between columns a and b is preferable and shows the difference between respondents and non-respondents. The differences are minor, except for the sector 'natural resources', which is over-represented among the respondents, and the sector 'accommodation and food services', which is under-represented among the respondents, accounting for only 5% of the respondents and 10.2% of the non-respondents. The number of non-respondents for natural resources, at 26 (761*.034), is small for a non-respondent survey, but it would be possible to conduct a small survey of the 78 (761*0.102) non-respondents in accommodation and food services, if there is other information to suggest that the respondents differ in important ways from the non-respondents.

Early versus late respondents
Research on the effect of non-respondents has often analysed differences between early and late respondents, on the assumption that late respondents will share similarities with those that never respond to a survey (Hendra and Hall, 2019). Early and late respondents can be identified through a gap in responses, for instance there could be a long lag between the second and third reminder letter, or the respondents could be divided between the first half to respond and the second half. The results for key variables should be compared between the early and late respondents to determine if there are statistically significant differences. For instance, a study on management methods could compare the share of early and late respondents for specific management activities.

Non-respondent survey
A non-respondent survey should be conducted as soon as possible after the end of the main survey and needs a high response rate, preferably over 80%. This is increasingly difficult to achieve, but the chances of success will improve if a suitable protocol is followed. To maximize response rates, non-respondent surveys should be conducted by telephone, take no more than two to three minutes of the respondent's time, and focus on a few key questions that are linked to the purpose of the survey. Since it is important to implement the survey on the first contact with a potential respondent, a non-respondent survey should use highly skilled interviewers who can get through receptionists (if present) and convince potential respondents to participate. The interviewer should stress that it will only take a few minutes to answer the questions and that their participation will be enormously helpful to the survey.

Table 6.2 gives an example of a short non-response survey that uses simpler versions of three key questions in the main questionnaire. The research question

Table 6.1   *Distribution of survey respondents, non-respondents, and the total sample by sector, average response rate 61.3%*

	a	b	c	d
Sector	Distribution of 1,204 Respondents	Distribution of 761 non-respondents	Distribution of 1,965 total sample	Response rate by sector
Natural resources	6%	3.4%	5%	73.5%
Financial, rental and information	8%	5.4%	7%	70.0%
Professional and administration	13%	10.4%	12%	66.4%
Manufacturing	23%	20.4%	22%	64.1%
Health care and social services	5%	5.0%	5%	61.3%
Transport and warehousing	5%	5.0%	5%	61.3%
Construction	10%	10.0%	10%	61.3%
Trade	20%	22.6%	21%	58.4%
Other services	5%	7.6%	6%	51.1%
Accommodation and food	5%	10.2%	7%	43.8%
	100%	100.0%	100%	

Table 6.2   *Example of a non-respondent survey*

In the last year, did your firm develop or improve any software, yes or no?				
Yes	☐	No ☐	Don't know (*do not prompt*)	☐

[*If 1 = yes*] In the last year, did your firm include free or open software code in any of the software developed or improved by your firm, yes or no?

Yes	☐	No ☐	Don't know (*do not prompt*)	☐

Does your firm hold one or more software patents in any jurisdiction, yes or no?

Yes	☐	No ☐	Don't know (*do not prompt*)	☐

concerns the effect of both open-source software code and patented software code on software innovation. The key characteristic of the firm is whether it develops software (if it doesn't it is not eligible for the survey). If firms pass this requirement, then the key characteristics are if they use open-source code and if they have a software patent. The 'do not prompt' for the 'Don't know' option reminds the interviewer to only use this option if reported by the interviewee.

Usually, a sample of 50 non-respondents is sufficient for a non-response survey. A more exacting estimate of the minimum size of the non-respondent survey is advisable if you expect respondents with characteristics of interest to your research to be more likely to reply than respondents without these characteristics, or if your study is designed to evaluate the effectiveness of a government policy or other type of intervention. Under these conditions, you should determine the ability of the non-respondent survey to detect a 'meaningful' difference in comparison to your respondents. For instance, a 20% difference between respondents and non-respondents on a key variable might be considered as a meaningful level of bias for the research questions. Use online software to determine the necessary sample size (section 5.5.3).

6.2.3   Data Editing (Cleaning)

Once the survey is closed and almost all expected questionnaires have been received (other than a few late returns), the data need to be 'cleaned', which involves checking the data and coding for errors, checking the variable names, addressing missing data, and running checks on response behaviours that can reduce data quality (section 3.9). Data cleaning can take between a few weeks and a month or longer. Before you begin cleaning the data file, it is essential to save the original master file and use different names for subsequent versions. This makes it possible to return to the master file if an error is accidentally introduced into the data during data cleaning. You should also save and rename versions as you work.

Flag variables

It is common for the values of many variables to be changed as a result of data cleaning, either to correct errors or to impute new values, as for variables with missing data. For all variables with changed values, add a new flag variable to the data file that identifies changed variables and the type of change. For instance, the original variable 'QA2a' could be accompanied by the flag variable 'FLAGQA2a' where the value equals 1 if QA2a is imputed, 2 if a change was made for a different reason, and 3 if the quality of the data is low, due to evidence of satisficing or other undesirable behaviour. In analysis, the flag variable will permit excluding QA2a if it is necessary to exclude imputed values or to check the difference in results with and without the exclusion of lower-quality data.

Checking data for errors

Errors can occur from the respondent entering illogical or ineligible responses into the questionnaire. Most of these can be prevented in an online format, but on a printed questionnaire a respondent could enter percentages that sum to over 100% or make a mistake when entering interval data for sales or the number of employees.

There can also be logical inconsistencies between questions. For instance, a respondent could report 1 billion Euros in sales and ten employees, or report zero exports in one question and positive export sales in another, or report no product innovations but sales from product innovations. For the sales example, the respondent may have made a mistake in entering the data, for example by adding an extra three zeros that changed the sales from a more logical 1 million. Producing frequency results for interval level questions can be used to identify outliers. Crosstabs can compare the results between two or more questions to identify logical inconsistencies in related questions (Leiner, 2019).

When errors are found, the first step for data obtained from printed questionnaires is to check the original questionnaire, as the error may have been created during data entry, or the answer may be difficult to read. If this is not the cause, the solution is either to contact the respondent or look at other variables in the data that provide evidence for interpretation. For instance, a respondent who reports no innovations in an early question, but reports innovation activities in a later question, is likely to have an innovation and incorrectly answered the early question. If the evidence is convincing, the value of the early question can be changed and the change noted in a flag variable.

Another error is when two responses are obtained from the same sampling unit. This can occur because the respondent answers a second time after a reminder, for instance they answer first to a printed version and a second time to an online version (or vice versa), or a second response is completed by a colleague on the original respondent's behalf. Repeats can be identified by searching the list of questionnaire IDs for questionnaires with the same ID number. If found, compare the two questionnaires and keep the version with the lowest number of missing values. If equal, keep the first one. The answers to a few questions may also differ between the first and second response, but only replace data that were missing in one questionnaire with data available in the other. Other attempts to guess at the best of two different responses could introduce your own biases into the data.

Always evaluate the written description in response to an 'other' option in a list question. For example, a list question on the types of services provided by a public sector agency could include seven types of services, such as 'educational services', 'health services', 'housing or urban services', etc., plus an 'other' option with space to write in a description. In many cases the written examples for the 'other' option are sufficient to reassign the response to one of the items in the list.

Variable coding
All coding should be checked to ensure that no errors were made, particularly for ordinal response categories that use numbers for 'low' to 'high' importance or another ordinal measure. More often than one might think a question can be

erroneously coded in the reverse direction, for instance '3' equals low importance when the intention was for '3' to equal high importance.

Variable names
Survey software can automatically generate long variable names. If you plan to use syntax files (a list of commands) to analyse the data, you will benefit from replacing long variable names with shorter names that are easy to type. Even if the statistical software has dropdown lists that permit pasting names into a syntax file, it is frequently faster to type short names than to search lists. In case errors force you to return to the original data, keep a log of manual variable name changes or the syntax file to automatically change variable names. A short name can include the section, question number and sub-question number. For instance, variable names for five sub-questions for question 2 in Section A could vary from QA2a to QA2e. Commonly used variables such as the number of employees can be given simple names such as 'employnum'.

Missing values
It is very common for a questionnaire to contain several missing values, where there is no response to a question (an item non-response). This will be more common in printed questionnaires than online questionnaires because the latter can provide a reminder when a question is missed.

For all survey types, the first step is to calculate the item non-response for all questions. This should be very low (less than 3%) for yes or no questions and low (less than 5% to 10%) for ordinal questions. The item non-response rate is usually higher for interval level questions. It can also increase for all types of questions located near the end of the questionnaire.

Missing values are a challenge because they can considerably reduce the number of cases available for multivariate analysis. Where feasible, missing values should be replaced with an imputed value and marked in the relevant flag variable. There are several approaches to estimating the unknown value of an item non-response. All approaches require careful evaluation and judgement.

Under some conditions a missing value can be assumed to equal zero or no or low importance, as in a matrix question. An example is given in Table 6.3. The respondent completed the questions for expenditures on the purchase of machinery and equipment and for the purchase of training services but left blank the questions for the purchase of research services and licences. The most likely value for these two questions is zero, with the respondent neglecting to fill in a value. An alternative explanation is that the respondent did not know the answer, but the expenditures would likely be very low, since the respondent was aware of a $5,000 expenditure on the purchase of design services.

Table 6.3   *Example of missing values for interval data*

In the last year, approximately how much did your business spend on the following types of purchases from other businesses:	
	Report in thousands of dollars (,000)
Purchase of machinery, equipment or technology	$_____150
Purchase of research services from other businesses	$_____
Purchase of training services from other businesses	$_____5
Purchase of licences to use patents	$_____

Consequently, changing the missing value to zero will either be correct or acceptably close to the true value.

For matrix questions, respondents may also skip question items of low importance. If there is only one missing value in a matrix question the respondent probably did not notice it, which is a true missing value. If multiple sub-questions were filled in, with several missing, the respondent may not have found the skipped activities to be important. It might be possible to assign these values as equal to 'low', but this is more likely to create errors than the example in Table 6.3.

Other imputation methods for missing values are to impute the value, using the nearest neighbour method, means or regression.

Nearest neighbour methods can impute missing values for nominal and ordinal data. The technique replaces the missing value with the response to the question by a 'nearest neighbour' donor case that is the most similar case to the recipient case on multiple characteristics, for instance a non-profit organization of comparable size, active in the same field, located in the same country, etc. The case should also share the same values for other relevant survey questions, such that differences between the donor and recipient case are minimized.

Assigning mean values is relevant to numeric variables. The mean value reported by other cases that share similar characteristics as the recipient case (sector, size, country, etc.) is calculated and used to replace the missing value in the recipient case.

Regression analysis can estimate missing numeric, nominal and ordinal data. The regression uses other cases in the data file and estimates an equation, using several variables collected in the survey that are known to predict the value of the variable of interest. For example, regression could be used to estimate revenue earned in the previous year, using data for variables that are known to influence revenue such as the number of employees, sector of activity, past capital investments, number of patents owned and innovation activity in the previous year. The values for each of these variables for the recipient case can be entered into the regression equation to predict the missing value for sales revenue. The problem with this approach is that it can predict unlikely results, such as negative values. All estimated values need to be checked to determine if they are plausible.

For each of the above three imputation methods, cases with imputed values for a dependent variable should be excluded from regression and other inferential statistical analyses because the imputed value is based on identified relationships between variables in other cases. This will artificially increase the correlation between the independent and dependent variables in statistical analysis.

Satisficing behaviour
The results for all matrix questions in both online and printed questionnaires should be checked for satisficing behaviour that results in giving the same response to all items in the question. This behaviour should be identified in the flag variable. This permits sub-questions in an affected matrix to be included and excluded during analysis to determine if exclusion makes a notable difference to the results. If the answer is yes, responses that have been affected by satisficing behaviour should be excluded.

Late respondents could give less thought to each question than early respondents. One study found that late respondents had higher item non-response rates than early respondents, but there was only weak evidence to suggest that the answers were less accurate and there were no differences in scale reliability (Olson, 2013).

Paradata collected in the main survey (section 5.7) can be used to identify respondents who rush or speed through the entire questionnaire. Very short survey completion times of less than half the average time is a strong marker of poor-quality data (Leiner, 2019; Revilla and Ochoa, 2014). In some cases, all data from speeders may need to be excluded during analysis.

Speeding can also be limited to a single question or a type of question. Affected questions can be flagged to enable a comparison of results with and without speeders. This method should not be used to assess factual questions as better-informed respondents will be able to respond more quickly (Leiner, 2019).

Speeders can't be identified in printed questionnaires. When the survey method uses both printed and online formats, it may be of interest to use paradata for online respondents to identify questions that are affected by speeding and to take this into consideration when evaluating results for all respondents. However, do not exclude only online cases affected by speeding for specific questions, since this may introduce bias.

6.3   OTHER ISSUES

Other issues that affect survey data include options for data linkage, data security, data anonymization, and validating results.

6.3.1   Data Linkage

Data linkage includes all methods of adding data from other sources to the survey database. Data can be available for individual sampling units, such as administrative microdata on the sales or number of employees for businesses, or for different aggregates of respondents. For example, a survey of multiple managers within municipal governments could include data for each municipality, such as a categorical variable for the population of the municipality (under 1,000, 1,000 to 9,999, 10,000 to 24,999, etc.) or the municipal budget. All respondents from the same municipality would be given the same values for population and budget. A commonly used aggregate variable is the geographical region, such as the local region, state or country.

Linking microdata is very advantageous, particularly when it provides information with a time lag or interval level data. Relevant data may be available from public data sources such as Dun and Bradstreet or Orbis, but the sampling units used in the survey and the public source must match. For instance, a survey of establishments will not match public data at the enterprise level. Care must also be taken to ensure correct matching, as many organizations share similar names, or an organization can have different subsidiaries.

6.3.2   Data Security

Ethics approval in many countries or government regulations can require the use of specific methods to maintain the security of data on individuals or organizations. The General Data Protection Regulation (GDPR) for the European Union permits personal data for scientific research to be kept for an undefined length of time if it is stored securely (Article 5.1.e). A safe interpretation of this rule is to separate contact information from questionnaire data and store the latter in a separate location. In some countries, ethics approval requires data to be securely stored for a defined period of time, such as for five years after analyses are completed, after which time the data must be destroyed.

Secure storage requires all confidential data to be kept on secure password-protected computers and encrypted. Confidential data in printed form, such as completed printed questionnaires, need to be kept in a secure, locked location.

Within your research group, you need to obtain a signed confidentiality agreement from all individuals who will have access to the survey microdata. Annex 6.1 provides an example that can be modified to meet national or other confidentiality regulations.

6.3.3   Data Anonymization

Growing interest in open data in many jurisdictions could require you to publicly provide anonymized data for use by other academics, as discussed in section 5.3.2. Anonymization can ensure confidentiality and permit the public release of data for non-commercial research. However, anonymization must be done very carefully. It must ensure that other users of the data cannot identify the individual respondent or their organization.

The first method is to remove all identifying variables that could be used singly or in combination to identify the respondent or their organization. Common identifying variables include the location (country, region, city) of the organization, the industry or main activity of a private sector organization or the primary function of a government agency, the number of employees, sales or budgetary data, and written descriptions, for instance the most important challenge faced by the organization or the most important innovation in the last two years, and all information on the respondent such as their job classification, years of experience, age, gender, etc. The questionnaire should also be reviewed carefully to identify any other questions that could be used for identification. Removing identifying variables can be an effective form of anonymization, but for many types of research de-identified survey data is of much less value than data that contains this information.

The second method, which can be combined with the first, is to transform variables. For example, interval level data on the number of employees can be replaced with ordinal data (fewer than ten employees, nine to 249 employees, 250 + employees). Other interval level data could be transformed to nominal data. For example, a question on new equipment expenditures could be converted to a yes/no variable, with any expenditures on new equipment equal to yes and no otherwise. Ordinal questions, such as those on an importance or frequency scale, can also be anonymized by replacing the result with the average for the three most similar organizations to the target organization.

Transforming variables using these methods will only provide an acceptable level of anonymization if there are four or more cases within any cell (for instance in a table) that could be constructed during analysis and which include potentially identifying information. In addition, for numeric variables, a single case in a cell cannot account for more than 70% of the average value of the cell. As an example, a cell reporting nominal data could be based on five potentially identifying variables: large firms (over 250 employees), in manufacturing, conducting R&D, exporting to foreign markets, and located in Denmark. This cell may contain four or more firms, but the replacement of 'manufacturing' with the 'pharmaceutical' sector, or the addition of a more detailed location variable (city or region), could result in the data in this cell being based on fewer than four cases. With fewer than four cases, a well-informed person could guess the identity of one or more of the firms. To be secure, this method requires expertise and sufficient analysis to determine that no combination of identifying variables will produce a cell with fewer than four cases or have one case that accounts for 70% of a numerical average.

If you are required to anonymize your data, you need to budget for adequate funding and time to ensure that your anonymization is secure.

6.3.4   Validating Results

Key indicators for data collected through surveys based on non-probability samples, or probability samples with low response rates, should be validated against other reliable data sources, if possible. For example, it may be possible to compare survey estimates of average sales in specific sectors against equivalent government administrative data, after adjusting for firm size. Data on the share of firms that applied for a patent could be validated against reports using patent data to produce similar indicators.

6.3.5   Respondent Report

A respondent report will be necessary if it was promised in the survey invitation letter. The report should be completed and sent to respondents as soon as possible after the data are cleaned. The report should be short (between ten and 30 pages), focus on results of interest and provide descriptive results. It might be worthwhile to include a section where the respondent can compare results with its peers. For example, if the survey covers academic, private and public hospitals, results could be provided for each hospital type. A good layout is to provide one colourful chart or figure per page with a brief written explanation. There is no need to include multivariate results. The report can be emailed to respondents to reduce costs or mailed if you only have a postal address. You can inform respondents by email about future publications in journals.

6.4   CONCLUSIONS

Analysis of survey data does not begin once data is collected. Instead, there is an interval of up to a month or longer when a non-respondent survey may be required, data edited and missing values imputed, or survey data linked to data obtained from other sources. These tasks require attention to detail and accurate report keeping. Additional tasks such as data anonymization, validation and preparing a respondent report can occur after data analysis begins.

It is essential to create flag variables to identify survey data that have been changed in any way or variables that may be affected by undesirable behaviour such as speeding. Flag variables permit analyses that exclude or include changed variables or variables affected by speeding.

Data editing is under the influence of Murphy's law – something will go wrong. It is essential to keep copies of the original data file before any changes and keep updated copies (saved under different file names) while working through the data editing process. When mistakes are made (as they will be), you will be able to return to an earlier, mistake-free version.

7.   Data analysis and reporting

7.1   INTRODUCTION

This chapter covers three topics that link data analysis and reporting to your questionnaire design and survey method: survey characteristics that may affect data analysis, such as the use of weighting and methods for dealing with 'don't know' responses and inter-rater variability in analyses; statistical models for multivariate analyses; and information on survey methodology to include in a journal publication. The discussion of statistical models only includes basic information that is required to make decisions on question design (Chapter 3). It does not describe how to apply statistical methods, for which there are multiple sources on descriptive and multivariate statistics to analyse survey data, including econometrics textbooks (Cameron and Trivedi, 2005; Nardi, 2018) or the Sage series on quantitative applications in the social sciences, which provides in-depth explanations of close to 200 statistical methods.

7.2   SURVEY CHARACTERISTICS AND DATA ANALYSIS

Several characteristics of the questionnaire or survey method may need to be considered in data analysis, including sample weighting, missing values and 'don't know' responses, common method bias, and selection from the use of filter questions.

7.2.1   Sample Weighting

Weighting refers to the use of the inverse of the sample fraction to weight respondents for analysis (section 5.5.1). For example, if the sample fraction is 0.2, the weight equals 5 (1/0.2), which means that each sampled case is equivalent to five cases in the sampled population. The sample weights can also be adjusted for the response rate. If the sample fraction is 0.1 and the response rate is 50%, the realized sample is 0.10 * 0.50 = 0.05. The weight is therefore 1/.05 or 20.

Simple random sampling that uses the same sample fraction never requires weighting when producing univariate estimates of population characteristics, such as means or frequencies, or for multivariate analyses such as regression. An example of descriptive analyses that do not require weighting when there is only one sample fraction is the percentage of science faculties with one or more patents or the mean number of patents per science faculty. Conversely, weighting by both the sample fraction and the response rate would be required for output estimates for the sampled population, such as an estimate of the total number of patent applications by universities.

When stratified sampling is used, weighting is required to produce univariate estimates such as frequencies or variable means for the population of interest (Solon et al., 2015; Winship and Radbill, 1994). The relevant weights need to be assigned to each case in the survey database. Most statistical software programs include variables that use assigned weighting values to weight the data for analysis. SPSS uses 'weight' while STATA uses the 'svy' function that adjusts for differences in the sample size per sampling strata.

When more than one sampling fraction is used, the decision on whether to weight data for multivariate analysis requires an evaluation of the purpose of the analysis. Weighting is not necessary if the criteria used to stratify the sample are related to the independent variables in the multivariate analysis (Winship and Radbill, 1994). For example, commonly used criteria for stratifying a sample are sector and size in studies of businesses. Weighting is not required if these two factors are used as independent variables in regression. Conversely, weighting produces better results with less error when the sampling factor is related to the dependent variable. An example is an analysis of the relationship between several independent variables and total sales when firm size (number of employees) is used to stratify businesses for sampling. This is because firm size is positively correlated with sales.

Other factors can affect the decision to use sample weights, such as heteroskedasticity (the standard error of the error terms varies by the value of the independent variables) or research on treatment effects, as in studies of the effect of policy interventions. These are specialized topics (see Solon et al., 2015) that are beyond the remit of this book.

7.2.2   Missing Values and 'Don't Know' Responses

As noted in section 6.2.3, missing values for specific questions are common in survey data and can be addressed by several imputation methods. Similar issues can apply to 'don't know' responses. The simplest method of dealing with 'don't know' responses is to exclude them from analyses that use the variable. However, this can result in a high percentage of excluded cases for regressions or factor analysis that use multiple variables, since a case with one 'Don't know' value out of ten variables may need to be excluded.

There are three options: impute 'don't know' responses following the methods described in section 6.2.3, include the 'don't know' responses in the analysis, for example as a separate response option, or make a logical assumption about its value. The latter is not feasible for some types of nominal or ordinal variables where it is impossible to identify a logical value for a 'Don't know' response. For example, there is no logical option for a 'Don't know' response to a list-based question for six types of collaboration partners. Conversely, for Likert importance questions measured on an ordinal scale and some types of nominal questions, a 'Don't know' response is closest to a 'zero' or 'low importance' response than to other response options. For example, a respondent asked to assess the importance of five collaboration partners in a matrix question could answer 'Don't know' to one of them. This 'Don't know' response can be assumed to be equivalent to the lowest option provided (low) on the assumption that the respondent would be aware of important collaboration partners. The same assumption can be made for a list of related nominal questions where the response options are 'yes', 'no' and 'don't know'. However, 'don't know' responses cannot be changed if this option is selected for all items in a list or matrix question. This is either satisficing behaviour or the respondent really does not know the answers.

It is good practice to conduct analyses both including and excluding imputed missing values and reassigned 'don't know' responses. In many cases the results will be similar when affected cases are included or excluded, but a closer look at the data may be warranted if there is a significant difference in the results. A closer look could identify a single variable that leads to the difference or find that imputed values are correlated with other factors.

7.2.3   Common Method Bias

Common method bias (or common method variance) is unlikely to be a problem with a well-designed questionnaire that has been cognitively tested and uses different measurement methods (section 3.5.6), but journal reviewers may expect to see the results of analyses to determine if common method bias is present.

A widely used method for detecting common method bias is Harman's one factor test (Fuller et al., 2016), which uses factor analysis to identify the amount of variance loaded on one factor. If this exceeds 50%, common method bias is assumed to be present, with a single factor explaining the majority of the variance. To calculate, use a factor test available in a statistical package, include all variables to be used in the multivariate analysis, and set the number of factors to equal 1. Fuller et al. (2016) identify other methods for detecting common method bias or variance.

If common method bias is detected in your data, Tehseen et al. (2017) cover statistical methods that can be used to control for it during analysis.

7.2.4   Selection Due to Filter Questions

Filter questions create one or more different groups of respondents for which data are missing for respondents that were filtered out. For example, you may be interested in the financial amount businesses invest to limit their fossil fuel use, measured as an interval level variable and used as the dependent variable in an Ordinary Least Squares (OLS) regression. Your questionnaire includes different strategies, drivers and activities to reduce such use, including a sizable number of questions on different types of eco-innovation activities. The data for these questions are missing for firms that report no innovation activities in a filter question. You can include non-innovative firms in some analyses of the effect of firm characteristics on business investment, but OLS analyses that include innovation activities will need to exclude non-innovative firms. This can create biased results if innovative firms have higher investments to limit fossil fuel use than non-innovative firms, which seems likely.

There are two solutions. The first is to minimize the use of filters in your questionnaire. For instance, instead of including a filter on whether the firm had innovation activities, ask all firms if they conducted several activities, including both innovative and non-innovative activities. Many questions can be revised in this way, but you may still need to ask some firms a series of questions for which their answer will be 'no'. This can annoy respondents and lead them to drop out. The other option is to use a statistical method for self-selection (the cause of the bias), such as Heckman's self-selection model. First, estimate the probability to be innovative on the whole sample and extract from the model the 'inverse Mills ratio'. Second, include the inverse Mills ratio as a control variable in the model limited to the sub-sample of innovative firms (Cameron and Trivedi, 2005).

7.3   MATCH BETWEEN QUESTIONS AND STATISTICAL METHODS

Multivariate statistics are available for small samples and for larger samples. Qualitative Comparative Analysis (QCA) or Partial Least Squares are useful for small samples, while larger samples can be analysed using Structural Equation Models (SEM) or different types of regression analysis.

The measurement level for the questions used to construct the dependent variable will determine the types of regression models that can be applied to survey data. Before you complete the design of your questions, it is worth thinking about the type of model you plan to use and if you can gather data at

Table 7.1 Appropriate regression models by the measurement level of the dependent variable

Measurement level	Models	Examples
Continuous interval data	Ordinary Least Squares (OLS)	Annual revenues
Interval with left or right censoring	Tobit	High or low values of the dependent variable are not available, for instance all values above one million are lumped together.
Interval count data with a large percentage of zero or 1 values	Poisson, negative binomial	Average number of patent applications for businesses in a specific year. A high percentage will report zero patents.
Ordinal	Ordered logit or ordered probit	Importance scales or small number of counts, such as the number of up to seven collaboration partners used by businesses.
Nominal (yes or no)	Logit or probit	An action or outcome is present or not (yes or no), or there is a choice of one of two options, one of which is defined as yes and the other as no.
Nominal with more than two options	Multinomial	More than two discrete options that do not overlap. A business could decide to develop a new employee safety policy entirely on its own, with the help of a major consulting firm, or with the help of a small innovation lab.

the necessary measurement level. You will need to collect interval level data for a dependent variable if you plan to use OLS. However, interval questions are often affected by a high item non-response rate of 40% or more that will seriously reduce data quality. An alternative is to link the survey data to an external source of interval data, but make sure that this is possible before you complete the design of your questionnaire, since confidentiality or other restrictions could limit your ability to access external data.

Another option is to use a different measurement level to collect data, such as an ordinal scale.

Changes to the measurement level, for instance from interval to ordinal, will require changing the statistical model. Whereas Ordinary Least Squares (OLS) can be used for interval level data, an ordered probit or logit model are appropriate options for dependent variables measured on an ordinal scale. Table 7.1 matches the level of data measurement for the dependent variable with appropriate multivariate regression models. This table is not exhaustive, only reporting commonly used statistical models to analyse survey data. For instance, OLS assumes a linear relationship between the independent and dependent variables, but non-linear models are also available for continuous interval data.

Two other possible characteristics of your data will require different statistical treatments that are available for many of the models listed in Table 7.1. If you have collected data at different points of time (panel data) you will need to adjust for these effects in your statistical model, but you may not need to collect additional information other than the date of each panel. Nested studies collect data at two or more levels. For example, data for multiple individuals within a sample of organizations has two levels: the individual level and the organizational level. The data collected from individuals within the same organization will not be independent because the organizational culture or rules could influence all respondents from the same organization to answer some of the questions in the same way. Consequently, you need to use multilevel (hierarchical) methods to control for this effect.

7.3.1   Non-random Samples, Censuses, and Large Samples

There are a few other important aspects of statistics to consider when conducting analyses and reporting results.

The calculation of statistical significance (the p value) assumes probability samples with random selection. Low response rates seriously constrain the value of descriptive results from probability samples, but the data obtained from samples with low response rates can be used for multivariate regression (Cornesse et al., 2020; Dassonneville et al., 2020).

Do not report statistical significance for descriptive results from a census with a high response rate. A census with a sampling fraction of 1 is not a sample and consequently statistical significance is meaningless. Any identified difference within groups in a census is a real result and does not require a test for statistical significance to determine if this effect would be identified by chance. It is up to you to decide if the differences are large enough to be meaningful.

Very large sample sizes, such as 5,000–10,000 cases or more, create a challenge because very small differences in two groups within the sample can be statistically significant. For instance, the sample could be large enough to detect a 2% difference at a probability of 0.05 or 0.01. Again, it is up to you to decide if this difference is meaningful. For regression models using census data, it is helpful to look at the marginal effects of the independent variables to identify meaningful variables.

7.4   WRITING UP YOUR METHODOLOGY FOR A JOURNAL ARTICLE

The reporting of survey methodology in many social science disciplines is poor. One study of 1,193 survey articles in business and management found that 23% did not give the response rate and 40% did not report the number of responses that were excluded due to incomplete data or other reasons (Mellahi and Harris, 2016). Often the methodological details given in an article or in a report are insufficient for assessing the quality of the study. The information provided in a paper should provide information on questionnaire testing, basic information on the survey implementation, and exact quotes of all questions used to construct variables.

Information on questionnaire testing should include whether cognitive testing was conducted and, if yes, the sample selection criteria for interviewees and the number of cognitive interviews conducted. A description of pilot testing should include the sampling method (random sample, purposive sample, etc.), the size of the sample and the adjusted response rate.

Basic information to report for the main survey includes the dates the survey was in the field, the reference period, the survey collection method (online, postal, etc.), the number and types of follow-ups (email, mail, etc.), the total number of questionnaires sent out, and the number of responses excluded because they were ineligible or because the respondent could not be reached. The adjusted response rate should be provided. Briefly describe research to detect differences in respondents and non-respondents if the response rate is less than 80%, including a non-respondent survey if conducted. If a stratified random sample is used, identify descriptive or multivariate results that use weighting.

Finally, include exact quotes of all questions used to construct all variables used in the article and provide a web link or other reference to the full questionnaire. Readers need to make their own judgement over your interpretation of survey questions. It is good practice to scrupulously follow what is said in the question and not to deviate by reinterpreting one or more questions to fit your research questions. Since this is your questionnaire, deviations should not be necessary.

7.5   CONCLUSIONS

Statistical issues such as the choice of a statistical model, common method bias, the effect of question filters, and the use of statistical probability need to be considered before completing the design of your questionnaire to minimize future problems during data analysis. In addition, journal articles based on survey data need to report full methodological information so that readers can assess the quality of your data.

8. Conclusion

This handbook covers all aspects of designing and implementing a questionnaire survey on the activities of organizations such as businesses, public sector agencies and non-governmental organizations. The chapters are also relevant to surveys on the perceptions or actions of individuals. The book discusses the initial steps of designing a questionnaire to answer research questions, through implementation and data cleaning, to the preparation of questionnaire data for statistical analysis.

Often, one of the first steps is to create a calendar time budget and a financial budget for a survey, particularly if you plan to apply for funding before you begin work on the first steps of writing a questionnaire. The various expenditure lines in a budget will give the impression that designing and implementing a questionnaire follows a sequential list of actions. This is not the case because many of the steps are interrelated. Statistical issues such as the choice of a statistical model, concerns over common method bias, and the effect of question filters need to be considered before completing the design of the questionnaire and survey methodology. This will minimize future problems during data analysis. Questions also need to be adapted to the survey method, which can be based on interviews, conducted online, or use printed questionnaires delivered by post. Ethics and confidentiality regulations will affect both the design of your questionnaire and data management.

These relationships between different parts of the survey require familiarity with all aspects of a survey, from questionnaire design to post-survey preparation of your data, before estimating a budget or beginning to design a questionnaire. The best preparation is to read the entire handbook, but, if short of time, Chapter 2 gives an overview of all activities that need to be considered as part of preparing budget estimates.

The goal of all surveys, whether of organizations or individuals, is to obtain high-quality data at a reasonable cost that are suitable for answering a set of questions. This requires a good response rate and an appropriate sample. Translating your research questions into questions that can be understood by all individuals in your sample is the first step should not be rushed. It requires a thorough understanding of the relevant literature and often considerable thought for how to put academic concepts into simple language.

Good practices for questionnaire design vary by survey method, with differences for 'heard' questionnaires (telephone or face-to-face interviews) and self-administered questionnaires that are read by respondents, either on paper or on a device such as a desktop/laptop, tablet or smartphone. You need to decide on the survey method before designing your questions. Given declining response rates to surveys, your questionnaire needs to be as short as possible, which means leaving out 'nice to know' questions. A key goal is to ensure that the questionnaire contains no more questions than are needed nor omits any necessary questions to answer research questions.

Questionnaire testing is essential for minimizing errors from respondents misunderstanding a question or being unable to provide an accurate response. In addition to asking peers to evaluate questions, a questionnaire must undergo cognitive testing with ten or more individuals drawn from the study population and, if funds are available, testing in a small pilot survey. Testing ensures that all questions can be understood as intended by all individuals in your sample and the data collected are of high quality, achieving content validity (the questions measure what the researcher wants to measure), inter-rater validity (questions are interpreted in the same way by different respondents) and reliability (respondents give accurate responses that result in very few false positives and false negatives).

Survey implementation requires careful preparation, attention to detail and a clear understanding of the research questions, which determine the population of interest and the estimated realized sample size. This is almost always the most expensive part of a survey and involves building a sample and delivering the survey. Costs will be considerably reduced if there is an existing database for the names and contact details of a sample of individuals to be surveyed. If not, careful and potentially expensive research is required to construct a sample. The cost of delivering the questionnaires to sampled individuals depends on the survey method. The least expensive option is to conduct an online survey, but due to low response rates it should be combined with another survey method, usually a postal survey using printed questionnaires.

Once the survey is completed, time is required to process the collected data before they are ready for analysis. This requires a non-respondent analysis to identify possible biases between respondents and non-respondents, and also data editing (cleaning) to check for errors, impute missing values, identify satisficing and other respondent behaviours that can reduce data quality, and construct flag variables to identify any variable that has been corrected or imputed.

Journal articles or reports based on survey data need to report full methodological information so that readers can assess the quality of the survey data.

Survey methods have changed considerably over the past two decades and are likely to continue to change in the future. An example is the rise in the use of the internet to contact sampled individuals, with respondents completing a questionnaire on a desktop or laptop instead of on a paper version. In the last decade, an increasing share of online respondents have chosen to complete surveys on their smartphone, requiring changes to question design and shorter questionnaires that take less time to complete. Researchers have been testing questionnaires online (web probing) to replace face-to-face cognitive testing, although this is still experimental. Greater familiarity with online video meetings because of the COVID-19 pandemic creates new options for conducting interview surveys and cognitive testing by video. These are exciting developments because they can considerably reduce the financial cost and time to conduct a survey.

Yet there is a sting in the tail – new methods may not be appropriate for all individuals in a sample, or they may collect more limited data, as in web probing or questionnaires designed for smartphones. It may be difficult in a video call to build rapport with an interviewee, an important element of cognitive testing. The best option for researchers is to use combined survey methods, such as an online/postal survey, that provide potential respondents with an alternative method of completing a questionnaire. Yet even this may change in the future, as all cohorts of the population become increasingly familiar and comfortable with online surveys.

Although new methods may offer many advantages, adopt them carefully. Make sure that there is sufficient research to establish that the method is effective for the types of individuals that you want to survey. For instance, extensive research on a new method among university students or a commercial panel is unlikely to be representative of middle or upper managers in a business or government agency. In addition, research on new methods should provide information on necessary changes to the questionnaire or the delivery method to obtain good results.

Finally, always remember Murphy's law: if something can go wrong, it will. Keep careful records. Back up all data files. Don't rely on recording interviews – recording devices will fail, whereas it is almost always easy to acquire a new pen for making notes if yours runs out of ink. Keep all originals of completed questionnaires and data in a secure place, and keep copies in a different secure place. Never put identifying information such as a respondent's name or company on a printed questionnaire or interview document. Murphy's law might cause you to inadvertently leave a completed form on a bus, train or in a rental car. Instead, use an identification number on documents that links to identifying information kept in a separate location.

References

Alvares, J., Campos, D.B., Zucoloto, M.L., Bonafe, F.S.S., Jordani, P.C. and Maroco, J. (2011). Reliability and validity of self-reported burn-out in college students: a comparison of paper and pencil vs. online administration. *Computers in Human Behavior* 27, 1875–1883.

Anseel, F., Lievens, F., Schollaert, E. and Choragwicka, B. (2010). Response rates in organizational science, 1995–2008: a meta-analytic review and guidelines for survey researchers. *Journal of Business and Psychology* 25(3), 335–349.

Arundel, A., Es-Sadki, N., Desmarchelier, B., Lagunes, H., Marton, K., Nordii, A., Rubalcaba, L. and Strokosch, K. (2019). Report D2.3, Report summarizing cognitive testing plus the final questionnaire, Co-Val, 1019. https://www.co-val.eu/wp-content/uploads/2019/06/0707F01_Report-summarizing-cognitive-testing-plus-the-final-questionnaire.pdf

Barge, S. and Gehlbach, H. (2012). Using the theory of satisficing to evaluate the quality of survey data. *Research in Higher Education* 53, 182–200.

Behr, D., Meitinger, K., Braun, M. and Kaczmirek, L. (2017). Web probing-implementing probing techniques from cognitive interviewing in web surveys with the goal to assess the validity of survey questions. Mannheim, GESIS – Leibniz Institute for the Socials Sciences. DOI:10.15465/gesis-sg_en_023.

Belfo, F.P. and Sousa, R.D. (2011). A web survey implementation framework: evidence-based design practices. Conference paper in the 6th Mediterranean Conference on Information Systems, MCIS 2011, Cyprus, 3–5 September.

Best, S.J. and Krueger, B.S. (2004). *Internet data collection* (No. 141). Sage.

Beullens, K., Loosveldt, G., Vandenplas, C. and Stoop, I. (2018). Response rates in the European social survey: increasing, decreasing, or a matter of fieldwork efforts? Survey methods: insights from the field. https://surveyinsights.org/?p=9673

Blair, J., Conrad, F., Ackermann, A.C. and Claxton, G. (1994). *The effect of sample size on cognitive interview findings*. Institute of Social Research, University of Michigan.

Bogen, K. (1996). *The effect of questionnaire length on response rates: a review of the literature*. US Bureau of the Census, Washington, DC.

Brosnan, K., Grün, B. and Dolnicar, S. (2017). PC, phone or tablet?: use, preference and completion rates for web surveys. *International Journal of Market Research* 59(1), 35–55.

Burns, G.N. and Christiansen, N.D. (2011). Methods of measuring faking behavior. *Human Performance* 24(4), 358–372.

Cameron, A.C. and Trivedi, P.K. (2005). *Microeconometrics: methods and applications*. Cambridge University Press.

Cho, Y.I., Johnson, T.P. and VanGeest, J.B. (2013). Enhancing surveys of health care professionals: a meta-analysis of techniques to improve response. *Evaluation & The Health Professions* 36(3), 382–407.

Cole, J.S., Sarraf, S.A. and Wang, X. (2015, May). Does use of survey incentives degrade data quality? Association for Institutional Research Annual Forum.

Collins, D. (2003). Pretesting survey instruments: an overview of cognitive methods. *Quality of Life Research* 12, 229–238.

Conroy, R.M. (2018). *The RCSI sample size handbook. A rough guide*. RCSI.

Converse, J.M. and Presser, S. (1986). *Survey questions: handcrafting the standardized questionnaire* (Vol. 63). Sage.

Cornesse, C., Blom, A.G., Dutwin, D., Krosnick, J.A., De Leeuw, E.D., Legleye, S., Pasek, J., Pennay, D., Phillips, B., Sakshaug, J.W. and Struminskaya, B. (2020). A review of conceptual approaches and empirical evidence on probability and non-probability sample survey research. *Journal of Survey Statistics and Methodology* 8(1), 4–36.

Couper, M.P., Kennedy, C., Conrad, F. and Tourangeau, R. (2011). Designing input fields for non-narrative open-ended responses in web surveys. *Journal of Official Statistics* 27, 65–85.

Couper, M.P., Tourangeau, R., Conrad, F. and Zhang, C. (2013). The design of grids in web surveys. *Social Science Computer Review* 31, 322–345.

Crawford, S.D., Couper, M.P. and Lamias, M.J. (2001). Web surveys: perceptions of burden. *Social Science Computer Review* 19(2), 146–162.

Curtin, R., Presser, S. and Singer, E. (2000). The effects of response rate changes on the index of consumer sentiment. *Public Opinion Quarterly* 64, 413–428.

Daikeler, J., Bošnjak, M. and Lozar Manfreda, K. (2020). Web versus other survey modes: an updated and extended meta-analysis comparing response rates. *Journal of Survey Statistics and Methodology* 8(3), 513–539.

Dassonneville, R., Blais, A., Hooghe, M. and Deschouwer, K. (2020). The effects of survey mode and sampling in Belgian election studies: a comparison of a national probability face-to-face survey and a nonprobability Internet survey. *Acta Politica* 55(2), 175–198.

Davis, D., Blair, J., Crawley, E., Craig, K., Rappoport, M., Baker, C. and Hanson, S. (2001). Census 2000 Quality Survey Instrument Pilot Test, Final Report, Development Associates.

Davis, W.L. and DeMaio, T.J. (1993). *Comparing the think aloud interviewing technique with standard interviewing in the redesign of a dietary recall questionnaire*. US Census Bureau.

DeMaio, T., Mathiowetz, N., Rothgeb, J., Beach, M.E. and Durant, S. (1993). *Protocol for pretesting demographic surveys at the Census Bureau*. US Bureau of the Census.

Dillman, D. (2000). *Mail and internet surveys: the tailored design method* (2nd edn). Wiley.

Dillman, D.A. and Smyth, J.D. (2007). Design effects in the transition to web-based surveys. *American Journal of Preventive Medicine* 32(5), S90–S96.

Dillman, D.A., Smyth, J.D. and Christian, L.M. (2014). *Internet, phone, mail, and mixed-mode surveys: the tailored design method*. John Wiley and Sons.

Dillman, D.A., Phelps, G., Tortora, R., Swift, K., Kohrell, J., Berck, J. and Messer, B.L. (2009). Response rate and measurement differences in mixed-mode surveys using mail, telephone, interactive voice response (IVR) and the Internet. *Social Science Research* 38(1), 1–18.

Dolnicar, S., Grun, B. and Yanamandram, V. (2013). Dynamic, interactive survey questions can increase survey data quality. *Journal of Travel and Tourism Marketing* 30, 690–699.

Downes-Le Guin, T., Baker, R., Mechling, J. and Ruylea, E. (2012). Myths and realities of respondent engagement in online surveys. *International Journal of Market Research* 54, 1–21.

Dykema, J., Stevenson, J., Klein, L., Kim, Y. and Day, B. (2012). Effects of e-mailed versus mailed invitations and incentives on response rates, data quality, and costs in a web survey of university faculty. *Social Science Computer Review* 31, 359–370.

Fan, W. and Yan, Z. (2010). Factors affecting response rates of a web survey: a systematic review. *Computers in Human Society* 26, 132–139.

Fink, A. (2003). *The survey handbook* (2nd edn). Sage Publications.

Forsyth, B.H. and Lessler, J. (1991). Cognitive laboratory methods. In P. Biemer et al. (eds), *Measurement errors in surveys*, pp. 393–418. Wiley and Sons.

Fowler, S. and Willis, G.B. (2020). The practice of cognitive interviewing through web probing. In P. Beatty et al. (eds), *Advances in questionnaire design, development, evaluation and testing*, pp. 451–469. John Wiley and Sons.

Fuller, C.M., Simmering, M.J., Atinc, G., Atinc, Y. and Babin, B.J. (2016). Common methods variance detection in business research. *Journal of Business Research* 8, 3192–3198.

Fulton, B.R. (2018). Organizations and survey research: implementing response enhancing strategies and conducting nonresponse analyses. *Sociological Methods & Research* 47(2), 240–276.

Galesic, M. and Bosnjak, M. (2009). Effects of questionnaire length on participation and indicators of response quality in a web survey. *Public Opinion Quarterly* 73(2), 349–360.

George, B. and Pandey, S.K. (2017). We know the yin—but where is the yang? Toward a balanced approach on common source bias in public administration scholarship. *Review of Public Personnel Administration* 37(2), 245–270.

Gobo, G. (2004). Sampling, representativeness and generalizability. *Qualitative Research Practice*, Sage, pp 435–456.

Grable, J.E. and Britt, S.L. (2011). An investigation of response bias associated with electronically delivered risk-tolerance assessment. *Journal of Financial Therapy* 2, 43–52.

Grady, R.H., Greenspan, R.L. and Liu, M. (2019). What is the best size for matrix-style questions in online surveys? *Social Science Computer Review* 37(3), 435–445.

Groves, R.M. (2006). Nonresponse rates and nonresponse bias in household surveys. *Public Opinion Quarterly* 70, 646–675.

Groves, R.M. and Peytcheva, E. (2008). The impact of nonresponse rates on nonresponse bias: a meta-analysis. *Public Opinion Quarterly* 72, 167–189.

Healey, B. (2007). Drop downs and scroll mice: the effect of response option format and input mechanism employed on data quality in web surveys. *Social Science Computer Review* 25, 111–128.

Hendra, R. and Hall, A. (2019). Rethinking response rates: new evidence of little relationship between survey response rates and nonresponse bias. *Evaluation Review* 43(5), 307–330.

Herzog, A.R. and Bachman, J.G. (1981). Effects of questionnaire length on response quality. *Public Opinion Quarterly* 45, 549–559.

Hiebl, M.R. and Richter, J.F. (2018). Response rates in management accounting survey research. *Journal of Management Accounting Research* 30, 59–79.

Hoogeveen, J. and Pape, U. (2020). *Data collection in fragile states: innovations from Africa and beyond*. Springer Nature.

Huang, H.-M. (2006). Do print and web surveys provide the same results? *Computers in Human Behavior* 22, 334–350.

Hughes, K.A. (2004). *Comparing pretesting methods: cognitive interviews, respondent debriefing, and behavior coding*. Statistical Research Division – US Bureau of the Census – Washington DC. 20233.

Jobe, J.B. and Herrmann, D.J. (1996). Implications of models of survey cognition for memory theory. In D.J. Herrmann et al. (eds), *Basic and applied memory research: practical applications* (Vol. 2), pp. 193–205. Erlbaum.

Kelfve, S., Kivi, M., Johansson, B. and Lindwall, M. (2020). Going web or staying paper? The use of web-surveys among older people. *BMC Medical Research Methodology* 20(1), 1–12.

Kim, Y., Dykema, J., Stevenson, J., Black, P. and Moberg, D.P. (2019). Straightlining: overview of measurement, comparison of indicators, and effects in mail–web mixed-mode surveys. *Social Science Computer Review* 37(2), 214–233.

Koen, B., Loosveldt, G., Vandenplas, C. and Stoop, I. (2018). Response rates in the European Social Survey: increasing, decreasing, or a matter of fieldwork efforts? *Survey methods: insights from the field*, pp. 1–12. https://surveyinsights.org/?p=9673

Kohut, A., Doherty, C. and Keeter, S. (2004). *Polls face growing resistance, but still representative*. Pew Center for Research on People and the Press, Washington, DC.

Kunz, T. and Hadler, P. (2020). *Web paradata in survey research*. Mannheim, GESIS – Leibniz Institute of the Social Sciences (GESIS – Survey Guidelines).

Lee, H., Kim, S., Couper, M.P. and Woo, Y. (2019). Experimental comparison of PC web, smartphone web, and telephone surveys in the new technology era. *Social Science Computer Review* 37(2), 234–247.

Leiner, D.J. (2019). Too fast, too straight, too weird: non-reactive indicators for meaningless data in internet surveys. *Survey Research Methods* 13, 229–248.

Lenzner, T. (2012). Effect of survey question comprehensibility on response quality. *Field Methods* 24, 409–428.

Lenzner, T. and Neuert, C.E. (2017). Pretesting survey questions via web probing: does it produce similar results to face-to-face cognitive interviewing? *Survey Practice* 10(4), 2768.

Lessler, J., Tourangeau, R. and Salter, W. (1989). Questionnaire design in the cognitive research laboratory: results of an experimental prototype. *Vital and Health Statistics* 6(1). (DHHS Pub. No. PHS 89-1076). U.S. Government Printing Office.

Liebe, U., Glenk, K., Oehlmann, M. and Meyerhoff, J. (2015). Does the use of mobile devices (tablets and smartphones) affect survey quality and choice behaviour in web surveys? *Journal of Choice Modelling* 14, 17–31.

Lindorff, M. (2010). Ethics, ethical human research and human research ethics committees. *Australian Universities' Review* 52(1), 51–59.

Medway, R.L. and Fulton, J. (2012). When more gets you less: a meta-analysis of the effect of concurrent web options on mail survey response rates. *Public Opinion Quarterly* 76, 733–746.

Meitinger, K. and Behr, D. (2016). Comparing cognitive interviewing and online probing: do they find similar results? *Field Methods* 28(4), 363–380.

Mellahi, K. and Harris, L.C. (2016). Response rates in business and management research: an overview of current practice and suggestions for future direction. *British Journal of Management* 27(2), 426–437.

Millar, M.M. and Dillman, D.A. (2011). Improving response to web and mixed-mode surveys. *Public Opinion Quarterly* 75, 249–269.

Müggenburg, H. (2021). Beyond the limits of memory? The reliability of retrospective data in travel research. *Transportation Research Part A: Policy and Practice* 145, 302–318.

Nardi, P.M. (2018). *Doing survey research: A guide to quantitative methods*. Routledge.

Neuert, C.E., Meitinger, K. and Behr, D. (2021). Open-ended versus closed probes: assessing different formats of web probing. *Sociological Methods & Research* p.00491241211031271.

Noel, V. and Prizeman, G. (2005). *Using cognitive question testing to pretest a questionnaire for a large-scale postal survey of nonprofit organizations*. School of Business Studies, Trinity College Dublin, Ireland.

OECD/Eurostat. (2018). *Oslo Manual 2018: Guidelines for collecting, reporting and using data on innovation, the measurement of scientific, technological and innovation activities*. OECD.

Olson, K. (2013). Do non-response follow-ups improve or reduce data quality? A review of the existing literature. *Journal of the Royal Statistical Society* 176, 129–145.

Peytchev, A. and Peytcheva, E. (2017). Reduction of measurement error due to survey length: evaluation of the split questionnaire design approach. *Survey Research Methods* 11, 361–368.

Peytchev, A., Conrad, F.G., Couper, M.P. and Tourangeau, R. (2010). Increasing respondents' use of definitions in web surveys. *Journal of Official Statistics* 26, 633–650.

Pinkse, J., Bohnsack, R. and Kolk, A. (2014). The role of public and private protection in disruptive innovation: the automotive industry and the emergence of low-emission vehicles. *Journal of Product Innovation Management* 31, 43–60.

Potaka, L. (2008). Comparability and usability: key issues in the design of internet forms for New Zealand's 2006 Census of Populations and Dwellings. *Survey Research Methods* 2(1), 1–10.

Presser, S. and Blair, J. (1994). Survey pretesting: do different methods produce different results? In P.V. Marsden (ed.), *Sociological methodology* (Vol. 24), pp. 73–104. Sage.

Qureschi, H. and Rowlands, O. (2004). User satisfaction surveys and cognitive question testing in the public sector: the case of personal services in England. *International Journal of Social Research Methodology* 7(4), 273–287.

Revilla, M. and Ochoa, C. (2014). What are the links in a web survey among response time, quality and auto-evaluation of the efforts done? *Social Science Computer Review*. DOI:10.1177/0894439314531214, May.

Rolstad, S., Adler, J. and Rydén, A. (2011). Response burden and questionnaire length: is shorter better? A review and meta-analysis. *Value in Health* 14(8), 1101–1108.

Sahlqvist, S., Song, Y., Bull, F., Adams, E., Preston, J. and Ogilvie, D. (2011). Effect of questionnaire length, personalisation and reminder type on response rate to a complex postal survey: randomised controlled trial. *BMC Medical Research Methodology* 11(1), 1–8.

Salant, P. and Dillman, D.A. (1994). *How to conduct your own survey*. John Wiley and Sons, Inc.

Saloniki, E.C., Malley, J., Burge, P., Lu, H., Batchelder, L., Linnosmaa, I., Trukeschitz, B. and Forder, J. (2019). Comparing internet and face-to-face surveys as methods for eliciting preferences for social care-related quality of life: evidence from England using the ASCOT service user measure. *Quality of Life Research* 28(8), 2207–2220.

Sammut, R., Griscti, O. and Norman, I.J. (2021). Strategies to improve response rates to web surveys: a literature review. *International Journal of Nursing Studies* 123, 104058.

Sandorf, E.D., Grimsrud, K. and Lindhjem, H. (2022). Ponderous, proficient or professional? Survey experience and smartphone effects in stated preference research. *Environmental and Resource Economics* 81(4), 807–832.

Sauermann, H. and Roach, M. (2013). Increasing web survey response rates in innovation research: an experimental study of static and dynamic contact design features. *Research Policy* 42, 273–286.

Saunders, M.N.K. (2012). Web versus mail: the influence of survey distribution mode on employee's response. *Field Methods* 24(1), 56–73.

Schaeffer, N.C. and Presser, S. (2003). The science of asking questions. *Annual Review of Sociology* 29(1), 65–88.

Shih, T.H. and Fan, X. (2008). Comparing response rates from web and mail surveys: a meta-analysis. *Field Methods* 20(3), 249–271.

Sikkel, D., Steenbergen, R. and Gras, S. (2014). Clicking vs. dragging: different uses of the mouse and their implications for online surveys. *Public Opinion Quarterly* 78, 177–190.

Sjöström, O. and Holst, D. (2002). Validity of a questionnaire survey: response patterns in different subgroups and the effect of social desirability. *Acta Odontologica Scandinavica* 60(3), 136–140.

Skeie, M.A., Lindhjem, H., Skjeflo, S. and Navrud, S. (2019). Smartphone and tablet effects in contingent valuation web surveys: no reason to worry? *Ecological Economics* 165, 106390.

Solon, G., Haider, S.J. and Wooldridge, J.M. (2015). What are we weighting for? *Journal of Human Resources* 50(2), 301–331.

Stedman, R.C., Connelly, N.A., Heberlein, T.A., Decker, D.J. and Allred, S.B. (2019). The end of the (research) world as we know it? Understanding and coping with declining response rates to mail surveys. *Society & Natural Resources* 32(10), 1139–1154.

Steiger, S., Reips, U.-D. and Voracek, M. (2007). Forced response in online surveys: bias from reactance and an increase in sex-specific dropout. *Journal of the American Society for Information Science and Technology* 58, 1653–1660.

Sudman, S. and Bradburn, N.M. (1973). Effects of time and memory factors on response in surveys. *Journal of the American Statistical Association* 68(344), 805–815.

Szolnoki, G. and Hoffmann, D. (2013). Online, face-to-face and telephone surveys—comparing different sampling methods in wine consumer research. *Wine Economics and Policy* 2(2), 57–66.

Tehseen, S., Ramayah, T. and Sajilan, S. (2017). Testing and controlling for common method variance: a review of available methods. *Journal of Management Sciences* 4(2), 142–168.

Thompson, S.K. (2012). *Sampling* (Vol. 755). John Wiley and Sons.

Toepoel, V. and Lugtig, P. (2022). Modularization in an era of mobile web: investigating the effects of cutting a survey into smaller pieces on data quality. *Social Science Computer Review* 40(1), 150–164.

Toninelli, D. and Revilla, M. (2020). How mobile device screen size affects data collected in web surveys. In P. Beatty et al. (eds), *Advances in questionnaire design, development, evaluation and testing*, pp. 349–373. John Wiley and Sons.

Tourangeau, R. (1984). Cognitive science and survey methods. In T. Jabine et al. (eds), *Cognitive aspects of survey methodology: building a bridge between disciplines*, pp. 73–100. National Academic Press.

Tourangeau, R. and Yan, T. (2007). Sensitive questions in surveys. *Psychological Bulletin* 133(5), 859–883.

Tourangeau, R., Sun, H., Yan, T., Maitland, A., Rivero, G. and Williams, D. (2018). Web surveys by smartphones and tablets: effects on data quality. *Social Science Computer Review* 36(5), 542–556.

Villar, A., Callegaro, M. and Yang, Y. (2013). Where am I? A meta-analysis of experiments on the effects of progress indicators for web surveys. *Social Science Computer Review* 31, 744–762.

Weigold, A., Weigold, I.K. and Russell, E.J. (2013). Examination of the equivalence of self-report survey-based paper-and-pencil and internet data collection methods. *Psychological Methods* 18, 53–70.

Willis, G. (1999). *Cognitive interviewing: a 'how to guide'*. Research Triangle Institute.

Willis, G. (2005). *Cognitive interviewing: a tool for improving questionnaire design*. Sage.

Willis, G. (2018). Cognitive interviewing in survey design: State of the science and future directions. In D.L. Vanette and J.A. Krosnick (eds), *The Palgrave handbook of survey research*, pp. 103–107. Palgrave Macmillan.

Willis, G., Schechter, S. and Whitaker, K. (1999). A comparison of cognitive interviewing, expert review, and behavior coding: what do they tell us? https://www.semanticscholar.org/paper/A-COMPARISON-OF-COGNITIVE -INTERVIEWING%2C-EXPERT-AND-Willis-Schechter/d5fbf351f75030d617a0 90123ce17902a72631fc

Winship, C. and Radbill, L. (1994). Sampling weights and regression analysis. *Sociological Methods & Research* 23(2), 230–257.

Zhang, X., Kuchinke, L., Woud, M.L., Velten, J. and Margraf, J. (2017). Survey method matters: online/offline questionnaires and face-to-face or telephone interviews differ. *Computers in Human Behavior* 71, 172–180.

Annexes

ANNEX 4.1   ROLE-PLAYING EXAMPLE FOR COGNITIVE TESTING

The 'interviewer' develops survey questions to answer a set of research interests as explained below under 'interviewer'. Three people play the role of company managers who the interviewer then interviews to cognitively test the questions.

Interviewer

You are very interested in how knowledge flows between private sector firms, including 'user innovation' where a firm builds on an idea developed by another firm or possibly an individual. User innovation is known to be common in sports equipment (surfboards, mountain biking, etc.) and in medical equipment, where a firm shares its knowledge with competitors. You expect that technology sharing will result in improvements that both firms can use. You are also interested if this also occurs for process innovation. It would help if firms are aware of the processes developed by their competitors. One question you have in mind is asking if firms have introduced a process innovation before any of their competitors. If they say yes, then they must know about their competitor's process activities. You have developed a question for this, but all of the people you have spoken to have said that firms won't know the answer because process innovations are kept secret.

Interviewee 1

You are the manager of a French firm with 700 employees that manufactures personal care products such as shampoo, soap and sunscreen. You sell products in eight countries. About 70% of your R&D budget goes on process innovation and the remainder on product innovation. Your firm recently collaborated with one other firm (an expert in organic coatings) and with a university (an expert on nanoparticles that absorb sunlight) to develop a new type of sunscreen based on nanoparticles. Your firm has also developed products in-house without collaborating. In your sector firms sometimes share their discoveries with other firms, but often they do not because of the high level of competition for personal care products. Firms in your sector carefully track what other firms are doing.

Interviewee 2

You are the manager of the European subsidiary of an American software firm, with 250 employees in Europe. Your firm is based in Switzerland and sells products throughout Europe, but you also conduct R&D on real-time language translation. As this is a fast-growing field there is a lot of sharing of information such as software code with other firms active in this area, but your firm rarely collaborates on innovation. However, there is a lot of technology sharing occurring informally. Your research unit has recently developed a new method that speeds up the coding process. You shared this information with one other firm in exchange for assistance from this firm with your firm's research on blockchains, but this wasn't sufficient. In the end you developed a new block-chain method with this other firm. In order to increase its market, both you and the other firm agreed to share this new method with your competitors.

Interviewee 3

You are the manager of a firm with 70 employees that makes disc brakes for bicycles. Your firm is based in the Netherlands, with sales in the Netherlands, the United States, France and Italy. You have never cooperated with other firms or universities for product development because of an intense fear of losing valuable intellectual property, but in the last year you contracted out some research work to Delft University to prevent brake slippage in wet weather. Delft University was able to solve the problem and provided your firm with a minor technical solution. It was difficult to develop a low-cost manufacturing process for this solution, but you did this entirely in-house to prevent your process from leaking to your competitors. In your sector you need to move fast once you introduce a new product onto the market because the first buyers of your new products will be your competitors, who will immediately reverse engineer your innovations. Your firm does the same.

ANNEX 4.2 INVITATION/INFORMATION SHEET FOR COGNITIVE INTERVIEWEES

Dear [Name]

I am writing to ask for your participation in an interview as part of research on the development of new or improved service innovations in the public sector. The study, [NAME], is funded by [NAME OF FUNDER], with participation by [list other participating organizations, if any]. The goal of [STUDY NAME] is to provide practical recommendations for how public sector organizations can improve the development and outcomes of their services. The project researchers include myself, [NAME] and [NAME] of [INSTITUTION].

Part of the [STUDY NAME] research involves a survey questionnaire on the methods that public sector organizations use to develop and implement services. The questionnaire asks about the use of information sources, the role of different drivers and barriers in developing services, and questions on how new or improved services are developed. In addition to [COUNTRY], the survey will be conducted in [NAMES OF OTHER COUNTRIES], with approximately [NUMBER] public sector managers in total receiving the survey questionnaire.

Survey questions first need to be tested in interviews with a small sample of potential respondents to ensure that the questions are understood as intended and that respondents can answer them with a reasonable level of accuracy. Many questions often fail this stage. As you can imagine, it is very important to identify problems with questions before they are included in a large survey.

You were identified as a potential interviewee by [EXPLANATION OF SOURCE]. If you agree to participate, the interview will be conducted by myself and [NAME] and can take place at your workplace. The interview will require approximately 45 to 60 minutes of your time. No sensitive information will be collected during the interview, since the focus is on your understanding and ability to answer a sample of questions. Your responses will be kept entirely confidential and no information will be reported that could be used to identify you or your organization. The results of your interview will only be used by project personnel for research on question design.

Your participation is entirely voluntary but would be highly valued and would help to ensure that the questionnaire will be correctly understood by potential respondents. We will contact you by telephone within a few days to ask if you are willing to participate. Even if you agree, you may still change your mind at any time.

Best regards,

[NAME]
[INSTITUTION]

[Ethics approval details if needed]

ANNEX 4.3   REMINDER EMAIL FOR A COGNITIVE INTERVIEW

[DATE]

Meeting reminder to participate in a study on improved public services

Dear [NAME]

This email is a reminder for our forthcoming meeting on [DATE and TIME] at [ADDRESS] to discuss proposed questions for a study on how public sector managers can improve their services.

If you need to change the date or time for this planned meeting, please contact me by email or by phone [TELEPHONE NUMBER].

Best regards,

[NAME]
[INSTITUTION]

[Ethics approval details if needed]

ANNEX 4.4   CONSENT FORM FOR [STUDY NAME]

1. I agree to take part in the research study named above.
2. I have read and understood the cover letter for this study.
3. The purpose of the study has been explained to me in person or in an information letter.
4. I understand that the study involves my participation in an interview about how I understand several questions on innovation and my views on the accuracy of my answers.
5. I understand that participation involves no foreseeable risks because none of my answers to the actual questions will be kept.
6. I understand that my answers on understanding and accuracy will be securely stored on the premises of [NAME of INSTITUTION] for five years and will then be destroyed.
7. My questions have been answered to my satisfaction.
8. I understand that the researcher(s) will maintain confidentiality and that any information I supply to the researcher(s) will be used only for the purposes of the research.
9. I understand that the results of this interview, if included in a publication, will be presented in such a way that neither myself nor [NAME of ORGANIZATION] can be identified.
10. I understand that my participation is voluntary and that I may withdraw at any time without any effect.

If I so wish, I may request that any data I have supplied be withdrawn from the research until [DATE].

Participant's name: _____

Participant's signature: _____

Date: _____

ANNEX 4.5   EXAMPLE OF INTERVIEWER AND INTER-VIEWEE QUESTION FORMATS FOR COGNITIVE TESTING

A. Interviewer

Service innovations

1. Were any of your branch's new or substantially changed services developed by:

(Tick all that apply)
  (a) Your branch mainly on its own   ☐
  (b) Your branch in collaboration[1] with others   ☐
  (c) Mainly other branches of your agency or other government organizations   ☐
  (d) Mainly other non-government organizations (businesses, consultants, etc.)   ☐

Note: [1]Collaboration requires an active role by your branch in the development of a new or substantially changed service. Exclude contracting-out or fee-for-service arrangements that do not involve input from your branch.

PROMPTS:
Ask them to define collaboration.
Did they read the definition of collaboration?
How did they arrive at their decision? Ask for examples for their responses.

2. Was your branch the first government organization in [country] to introduce any of these new or substantially changed services?

It does not matter if the service was already provided by government organizations outside [country] or by businesses inside or outside [country], as long as your branch was the first government organization (National, state or local) in [country] to provide them.

(Tick one box only)
  (a) Yes   ☐
  (b) No   ☐
  (c) Don't know   ☐

PROMPT: Ask how they know. How accurate is their response? If no, are they aware of other government organizations that introduced a 'Country first' innovation.

B. Interviewee

1. Were any of your branch's new or substantially changed services developed by:

(Tick all that apply)
   (a)   Your branch mainly on its own   ☐
   (b)   Your branch in collaboration[1] with others   ☐
   (c)   Mainly other branches of your agency or other government organizations   ☐
   (d)   Mainly other non-government organizations (businesses, consultants, etc.)   ☐

Note: [1]Collaboration requires an active role by your branch in the development of a new or substantially changed service. Exclude contracting-out or fee-for-service arrangements that do not involve input from your branch.

2. Was your branch the first government organization in Australia to introduce any of these new or substantially changed services?

It does not matter if the service was already provided by government organizations outside Australia or by businesses inside or outside Australia, as long as your branch was the first government organization (Commonwealth, state or local) in Australia to provide them.

(Tick one box only)
   (a)   Yes   ☐
   (b)   No   ☐
   (c)   Don't know   ☐

Continue with question 3 on same page.

ANNEX 5.1   SURVEY CONTACT LETTER

[Institutional letterhead]
[DATE]

Study on new or improved services in public organizations

I am writing to ask you to participate in an online survey on the introduction of new or improved services by public sector organizations. The survey was developed by [NAMES of INSTITUTIONS]. The research is funded by [NAME OF FUNDER].

The survey asks if your organization has introduced any new or improved services in the past two years and the methods that your organization uses to develop and implement services. The survey is also relevant to organizations with no new or improved services.

The purpose of the survey is to support government policies and programmes across Europe with the goal of improving public services.

The survey will take approximately 15 minutes of your time. Your response is completely voluntary and anonymous. No information will ever be publicly released that could be used to identify yourself or your organization.

Within a few days you will receive an email from myself with a confidential link to the survey. The subject line for the email will state '*Survey on new or improved services*'. If you change your mind after submitting the completed survey, you may still request, via email, that your results be deleted.

In appreciation for your participation, you will receive a report of the main results by [DATE]. We hope that you find these results both interesting and helpful for future planning and development of services.

If you would like more information on this survey, please contact [NAME] at [TELEPHONE NUMBER] or send an email to [EMAIL ADDRESS].

[Signature]
[Name and title]

[Ethics approval number if necessary]

ANNEX 5.2 EXAMPLE OF A FIRST AND SECOND REMINDER LETTER

Example of a First Reminder Letter

[Institutional letterhead]
[DATE]

Reminder to participate in the survey on new or improved services in public sector organizations

Dear [Name]

Approximately two weeks ago we contacted you to ask if you would participate in a short online questionnaire survey on new or improved services in public sector organizations. To date we have not yet received your questionnaire and would like to remind you about this survey and its importance. However, if you have recently completed the survey, please ignore this email.

The survey was developed by [NAMES]. The findings of the survey will help public sector organizations to improve the methods they use to provide better services to other government organizations or to citizens.

The survey should only take approximately 15 minutes of your time. No personally sensitive questions are asked. All information provided will be kept strictly confidential. No results will be publicly released in any form that could be used to identify yourself or your organization. If you participate, you will receive a summary report of the main results in [DATE].

You can reach the survey by clicking on this link: [hyperlink]. Your password for access is [password].

If you have any questions about the survey, please contact myself or [NAME] at [NAME OF INSTITUTE] on [TELEPHONE NUMBER] or via email at [EMAIL ADDRESS].

With best wishes,

[Contact name]

[Ethics approval number if necessary]

Example of a Second Reminder Letter

[Institutional letterhead]
[DATE]

Reminder to participate in the survey on new or improved services in public sector organizations

Dear [Name]

We would still very much like a reply from you to our short online question-naire survey on new or improved services in public sector organizations. The results should help public sector organizations to improve the methods they use to provide better services to other government organizations or to citizens.

Please respond to the survey even if you do not believe that your organization has introduced a new or improved service in the last two years.

The survey should only take approximately 15 minutes of your time. All infor-mation that you provide will be kept strictly confidential, with no results ever released in any form that could be used to identify yourself or your organiza-tion. If you participate, you will receive a summary report of the main results in [DATE].

You can reach the survey by clicking on this link: [hyperlink]. Your password for access is [password].

If you have any questions about the survey, please contact myself or [NAME] at [NAME OF INSTITUTE] on [TELEPHONE NUMBER] or via email at [EMAIL ADDRESS].

With best wishes,

[Contact name]

[Ethics approval number if necessary]

ANNEX 6.1   CONFIDENTIALITY AGREEMENT FOR THE USE OF [SURVEY NAME], DATA FILE [NAME], [DATE], COLLECTED OR OWNED BY [NAME OF INSTITUTION].

I, _____ agree to the following confidentiality criteria for use of the above-mentioned survey microdata.

1. I agree not to give a copy of any of the microdata, in whole or in part, in any format (in paper, by email, in digital form, etc.) to any other person.
2. I agree not to permit any other person to have access to the data for the purpose of analysis or for any other reason, except for persons who already have a confidentiality agreement with [NAME of DATA OWNER] for the use of this data.
3. I agree not to present any results or any part of the data in such a way that any person could identify an individual organization, responding unit or respondent. Presentation of the data includes oral, written, electronic or any other form. Under normal use, this means that any cell (as in a table giving descriptive results) must be based on a minimum of four responding units. Under some conditions (as when over 70% of the item in a cell is due to only one respondent) this limitation may not be adequate and I agree to use stricter limitations as necessary.
4. I agree to give a copy of all results for publication or presentation, in any location or format, to the [NAME of DATA OWNER] representative for pre-clearance.
5. I agree to keep the data on a computer that is protected by a secure password and not to upload the data to the cloud or other server. I agree to keep a separate back-up copy of the data on a single memory stick that is kept in a secure locked location (drawer, cupboard, etc.).
6. Once the analyses are completed, I agree to destroy the data files after two years.
7. I agree to take all necessary precautions in addition to those noted in points 1 through 5 to maintain data confidentiality.

Signed: _____ Date: _____   Location: _____

[NAME of DATA OWNER] representative:
[NAME]_____

Signed: _____ Date: _____   Location: _____

Index

Printed and bound by CPI Group (UK) Ltd, Croydon, CR0 4YY

16/04/2025

14658493-0003